D1539127

AND AGAIN, IT'S YOU

AND AGAIN, IT'S YOU

a memoir

JESSICA SHORSTEIN

First Edition

Cover Art by Bailey McGinn
Cover Photography by ReAnna Nicole Photography
Typesetting by Danna Mathias Steele
Editing by Shelby Newsom

ISBN: 979-8-9855388-0-9 (paperback)
ISBN: 979-8-9855388-1-6 (ebook)

www.jessicashorstein.com

HEART SHAPED PARK
PRESS

For Daniel (it was always you),
J, R, & E – my entire world.

For Bernard Grand who, for me,
will always be synonymous with New York.

CHAPTER ONE

Airplane Boy

THE LARGE, OPEN ROOM HUMMED WITH THE light energy of idle teenage chatter. The dinner plates and silverware had been cleaned from the rows of long, white, plastic-covered tables, one of which now held several large round platters covered with non-dairy kosher cookies. The sun had long ago set, and the room was aglow with a particular ineffable warmth that I only ever felt after attending a Jewish Shabbat service followed by dinner. This sentiment of relaxation, contentment, and an awareness and understanding of my place in the world was heightened by the fact that this was a Friday night in a hostel in the Negev, the desert of Israel. Being in Israel on the Sabbath made me feel as though I was in the exact place that I was supposed to be at this particular moment in time. It also called to mind the observance of all of the generations before me, who chanted the same prayers, sang the same songs, and felt a connection to this same place. When I breathed in the Israeli air, it was as though I could taste the history of my ancestors, and my past, present, meaning and purpose were all at once before me.

It was the summer of 2000, and I was seventeen and traveling through Israel with a Jewish summer teen tour group, the United Synagogue Youth (USY) Israel Pilgrimage. The patchwork of sixty girls and boys from all across the U.S. and Canada plus several staff members that made up my group may have been a random assignment, but I knew that the formative experiences we were sharing in this special country would not only define this whirlwind summer but would stay with me indelibly into the future.

For a several-day long stretch, my group had joined another USY Pilgrimage trip at this particular hostel in the desert. Thus far, we had spent most of our tour across the holy land in the company of only each other. Occasionally we would cross paths with another cohort, and we would nod and smile at one another on our way into or out of a historical site. Staying in a hostel for a night or two with another group was rare, though, and therefore exciting. And the peaceful calm that had been ushered in by Shabbat set the perfect scene to find someone new to flirt with over kosher cookies.

I stood in a small circle with some fellow girls from my group and eyed the underwhelming flat round cookies, debating whether my interest in reaching for one derived more from boredom or actual hunger, when I caught a glimpse of a boy on the other side of the room. He was several long, plastic-covered tables away from where I stood, and I felt my face warm slightly as my eyes lingered on him. I was taken aback by his handsome appearance—he didn't look like he belonged in this room of mostly awkward teenagers—he was too attractive, too composed, his smile too assured. He was the best-looking boy I had ever seen, whether at home in Pennsylvania, here in Israel, or anywhere. His close-cropped brownish-blond hair was made up of very tight curls that looked soft but somewhat spongy, like they might spring back slightly in response to being touched. His distinctive hair complemented his well-tanned skin and broad, dimpled smile. That would have been enough for me—*dayenu,* as we say during Passover Seders—but this boy also had large, gray-blue eyes that shone with an arresting blend of confident mischievousness and a deep sincerity. And—*dayenu*—but his sunny features were offset by a broad, strong build and chiseled face. It was as though an artist had sketched an image of this boy before declaring, "Here is what a young man should look like," and then the figure had magically sprung to life off that page, and now stood before me somehow in this room, on this night.

I finally turned away blushing, and then my eyes immediately darted back over to where he was standing, talking in his own small circle of friends. *Who is this guy?* What astounded me the most as I took in this person, in addition to the fact that he appeared to be real, was the fact that he was clearly also Jewish; he would not be in this room if he was not. But he did not look like most of the other Jewish boys I knew; his eyes and hair were lighter, which also meant that he was exactly my type.

I had heard about love at first sight. It was something that I believed in; I was well-versed in the popular romantic comedies of the 1990s, and my romantic self always believed it was possible. Looking now at this boy across a room bathed in Shabbat afterglow, and in Israel, a place that somehow felt like home to me, it felt as though I was in a scene from a movie of my own. The previous weeks of fast-paced travel throughout the country quickly flashed before me like a series of snapshots until suddenly there was only stillness, and in my mind the room was quiet now, the entire space blurred into the background of this boy because everything else was now merely a backdrop, a scene set specifically so I could notice him, and then we could meet.

"We need to go talk to that guy," I told my friends, who immediately knew what I actually meant by "we" was "I, with backup."

I wasn't afraid to approach him, albeit with an entourage. On this trip, I felt in my element. One of my three brothers, Mike, younger than me by only sixteen months and like a best friend to me, and Leah, another best friend, were both in the group with me, providing an inherent sense of comfort and the freedom to be myself. And something about being in Israel somehow brought out a more confident version of me, as though feeling connected to where I had come from and what I believed put into clearer relief who I was.

So the small group of us not-so-casually clambered past the rows of folding chairs and around a couple tables to where this boy, this being, this creation, was standing. One of my friends struck up a conversation with someone from his cluster, and soon we were all chatting. I had strategically placed myself just in front of this gentleman of intrigue so I could talk to him, and now I felt heat on my cheeks as he looked at me.

"Hi, I'm Jared," he said, flashing that smile directly at me, nearly paralyzing me where I stood.

It felt as though I was looking directly at the sun, frozen by the brightness and beginning to lose my bearings, but then, as I quickly studied his face and looked into his eyes, I saw that it was sincerity he offered, not intimidation.

I exhaled and smiled back. "I'm Jessica."

"So, enjoying your stay in the desert?" he asked with a playful look in his eyes.

I grinned again. "Yeah, it's been amazing. It's cool seeing your group here. We spend the whole summer with the same people."

He was still smiling and looking directly into my eyes as though nothing or no one else around us mattered. "I hear you. It's nice to change it up."

There was a short pause as he continued to look at me unfalteringly, his ocean eyes now sparkling with a mixture of curiosity and intrigue.

"So, have you ridden a camel yet?"

I felt myself continue to blush as Jared and I talked. We had a nice banter going now, but the words we were saying did not matter nearly as much as the fact that we were standing across from each other talking and flirting as I occasionally wondered if he noticed the flush on my face.

We were connecting, and there was a palpable chemistry between us, as though the air had been ignited and now crackled with a new electricity. I felt illuminated inside in a way I had never felt before. I heard conversations going on around me, but I wanted nothing else but to have more of whatever was happening just in front of me.

"Jess, we're heading up," I heard someone say to my right.

I turned my head in that direction, and as though I were snapping out of a trance, I suddenly saw Leah's face take shape next to me. I looked around and realized that there were now only a few people left in the room. It was time to go.

"OK, I'm coming now," I said quickly. I looked back at Jared and smiled. "It was great meeting you. Jared, right?"

He nodded slowly. "Indeed. Likewise, Jessica. Goodnight."

He beamed at me one more time, and for a second it felt like we should hug, but I held back as I realized that didn't seem like it would make sense, so I pulled myself away as if removing myself from a magnetic field.

I felt like I was dancing on air as I made my way out of the dining area with my friends and climbed through the stairwell back to my room. It now felt even more as though I was exactly where I was supposed to be on that night, in that moment. I was in Israel. It was the Sabbath. And I had just connected with the cutest boy I had ever seen, and we had hit it off, to boot. I felt different somehow, as though the dry desert ground beneath me and below the hostel had shifted slightly. It almost didn't matter what happened next because in this instant, I felt utterly content. But I hoped that was not the last that I saw of Jared. I wanted more of whatever that was.

———————

THE NEXT MORNING, I WALKED THROUGH THE bustling hostel lobby with my group, on our way back from a buffet breakfast of Israeli salad, eggs in various forms, and pastries. Since it was still Shabbat, the day of rest, there was little programming scheduled, and we could essentially do as we pleased. As we made our way toward our rooms, I saw Jared's group approaching us en masse on their way in to eat. Teenage heads bobbed up and down as we passed beside them, our cohorts running in opposite directions like busy lanes of traffic, and my eyes quickly scanned the moving crowd for close-cropped, curly hair.

I saw Jared just as he was about to pass right by me. As my eyes met his, I involuntarily averted my own. By the time he had approached me, I glanced back in his direction just as I felt his hand reach out and tickle my stomach, gently and clandestinely. He was already past me by the time I could process what had happened, then I smiled to myself. It had been such a subtle, fleeting action that none of the hordes of faces around us had seen. I was enveloped by a tingly, butterflies-in-my-stomach sensation, and I felt special, singled-out, chosen. *He likes me too.*

———————

"DO YOU WANT TO HEAD DOWN TO THE LOB-by? I think there's some people hanging out," Leah asked me as I sat on my hostel bed.

I thought of Jared. "Yeah, that sounds great," I said quickly.

It was the afternoon now, and we still had several hours left of free time at the hostel. I knew that Jared's group was around doing the same thing, and I was excited about the opportunity to talk to him again. I walked over to the small mirror on the tiled wall of the adjoining bathroom and peered at my face. I smoothed my hair back and quickly applied a new coat of lip gloss. I gave myself one last look, then I couldn't suppress a small smile as I thought about my secret exchange with him in the lobby that morning.

Before long, I was downstairs strolling around with Leah, surveying the tableaux of girls and boys standing or sitting together in small groups on the faux-leather lobby furniture. We had no destination in particular; we wandered about simply to see and be seen. I surveyed the room for Jared, all the while attempting to appear casual and as though I was not looking for something, or someone. When I couldn't locate his sandy, curly hair in the crowd, I decided with disappointment that he might have chosen to rest in his room instead of coming downstairs.

Just then, my gaze fell on a hallway leading from the lobby toward the hostel's kitchen, which I knew would be empty outside of meal hours. But I saw two figures walking down the corridor, and I recognized Jared immediately from behind; no one else had hair quite like his. He was walking hand in hand with a girl I did not know. I watched, stunned, as they disappeared around the corner and into the kitchen, alone. I stood in place staring at the empty hallway, no longer caring if it was obvious to anyone around me what I was looking at. *I thought he liked ME.*

I blinked and thought back to the night before when I had noticed him across the room, how it had felt like genuine love at first sight. I remembered how we talked and how it all felt so symbiotic, so correct to be connecting with him, and how special it felt when he secretly acknowledged me in the lobby the next morning. Our story had just begun. And now, as my stomach sank with the realization that he and that girl probably weren't going into the kitchen to find a snack, it just felt unfair. My interactions with Jared had given me the sense that I was living life on a higher, more energized plane, and I was left yearning for more. But it was evident now that I was just one of many objects of his flirtations.

I felt anger begin to rise inside me even though I knew he didn't owe me anything. We had barely interacted, but I was certain I couldn't have imagined a connection that palpable. I sighed. I saw Leah looking in the same direction as me, then I realized she had seen what I saw. She shook her head and took my hand, guiding me toward some boys from our group sitting on a nearby array of couches.

"Whatever," I said. "Let's go."

I still didn't even care that my emotions were apparent to the several others around us. I glanced back down the hallway one more time as we walked away. *Well, now he's missed his chance with me.*

In my mind, I felt a cool gust of wind slamming shut the hard cover of the beautiful love story we had just begun to write. I imagined taking it in my hands and placing it on a high shelf, squeezed in between a row of old volumes with dusty covers, and I knew that was where it would remain. I was determined to write Jared off for the rest of the summer. I knew I would likely only run into him a handful more times anyway, if even that, before our trips ended in a few weeks. Our exchanges had felt so significant to me, but if he wasn't even on the same page, then what was the point?

Between the friends who had been with me when Jared and I had met and so obviously hit it off and the others who had just witnessed the scene by the kitchen hallway, I was sure word would get back to Jared that I saw him with the other girl. Plus, I knew that one of the guys in my group was friends with him, and that if I told the guy how I felt, then in the natural course of things, it would make its way back to Jared. I carefully avoided him for the rest of our stay at the shared hostel, well aware that my coldness was not lost on him.

———

EVENTUALLY THE SIX FORMATIVE, UNIVERSE-EX-panding weeks that I spent traveling across Israel came to an end, and I sat on the return flight home. I had heard a rumor that the plane was also going to include members from other groups who had traveled through Israel at the same time, including Jared's. After the hostel in the desert, our cohorts had crossed paths only one more time, on a busy street corner in downtown Jerusalem. When I saw him walking toward me, I had avoided eye contact and made sure he didn't get close enough to me to try and start a conversation. What else was left to say?

I knew that this was about to be a long flight, somewhere in the ballpark of thirteen hours, and I wondered if I would see him on the plane. As I settled into my aisle seat next to my brother, I exhaled deeply, feeling bittersweet about the summer coming to an end and anxious to see the rest of my family back home in Pennsylvania. I turned around to see who else had sat nearby. As I glanced behind me, I felt my stomach drop as I saw Jared right away, just a few rows back and across the aisle. *Of course.* I accidentally caught his eye; it was unavoidable. I swiftly snapped my head back around and felt my face flush. In spite of myself, it was exciting to see him. I hadn't looked into his eyes since that morning at the hostel when we had shared that fleeting touch, before I saw him go off with that girl and everything had changed. I then recalled the hurt and anger I had felt in that moment seeing them disappear into the kitchen. I sighed. *Well, this will be fine. I just won't turn around for the next thirteen hours.*

The plane took off, and as I watched the dense white clouds pass outside the window, I thought about everything I had experienced that summer. I hoped to carry it all with me moving forward, like a locket around my neck that I could open to revisit a memory any time I wanted. I heard the pleasant "ding" of the fasten seatbelts sign clicking off, immediately followed by a chorus of metallic clicks as the restless girls and boys around me unfastened their seatbelts and began to move throughout the plane to say final farewells to their friends. All of a sudden, I felt a light tap on my arm from someone behind me in the aisle. I turned and saw Jared crouched down next to me. Any pride or resentment that I had been determined to hold onto moments before quickly dissipated as I was disarmed by his blinding, megawatt smile. I felt my face inadvertently warm.

"Hey, fancy seeing you here," he said. "So where is home?"

As I told Jared about the town in Pennsylvania where I grew up, I noticed how physically close to me he was as he knelt beside me in the aisle. I felt singled out and special in the way that I had when he passed me that morning in the hostel lobby, and I was eminently aware of the curious eyes around us now. The charming way Jared was speaking to me combined with the deep sincerity in his blue-gray eyes made it impossible to have any remaining hostility toward him. He told me about where he was from in Queens, New York. As we talked, I again felt the molecules in the air around us light up with the same distinctive chemistry from the night we had met. Once more the words that were said between us did not matter because again I felt a sense of elation, hope, and anticipation about what might happen next.

The atmosphere between us was lighter now that my fortress walls had crumbled into dust on the blue-carpeted airplane floor, so I readily handed Jared my USY Pilgrimage yearbook when he gave me his to sign. When he returned it to me before making his way back toward his seat, I was immediately left wanting to see him again, to talk to him again, so that I could simply experience that feeling once more, that sensation of equal parts giddiness, promise, and contentment. I opened up my yearbook, anxious to see what he had written. There was a short, friendly message, and following his signature, he had written his AOL Instant Messenger (AIM) screen name. I felt my face warm again. *He wants to stay in touch.* I looked at his screen name, Gr8tefulDd1023, a magic combination of letters and numbers that spelled Jared into my future beyond Israel. I smiled to myself as I imagined chatting with him late at night like I did with my other friends back at home. I didn't even wonder about whether or not we would stay in touch, or whether I would be able to experience that incredible feeling again. It felt like a certainty.

Still basking in the glow of the moment I had just had with Jared, I momentarily forgot that others around me had witnessed it. Suddenly my brother's voice pierced my reverie.

"Hey, who was that GUYYY? Do you LIKE HIM??"

I realized that I wasn't the only one who had noticed how close Jared was to me when he had crouched down in the aisle next to my seat. I smiled again.

"He's just a friend."

I knew he was more than that to me somehow, which was also apparent to my brother, who knew me well. I settled into my seat again, now soaring with a new excitement about what was to come after the airplane descended back onto the earth and I returned home.

———————

THE SUN WAS SETTING OVER THE LAKE OUTside the windows of my family's summer cottage in rural Pennsylvania as I sat down in front of our shared laptop that was open on the round kitchen table. A warm yellow-orange glow shone from two lights over my head that had been dimmed to complement the late hour. I had successfully managed to fend off all of my brothers for a chance at the computer, and I couldn't wait to log into AIM so I could add Jared to my Buddy List and see if he was online. Despite my nervous and excited anticipation, I had to wait patiently as the computer worked to get online through our dial-up connection. I exhaled deeply when I heard the sweet and satisfying "eeeeerrrrr EEEEEEeerrr eeeeeeeer eeerrrr sssshhh shhh-shhaaaaaaa…." as a connection was made.

My USY Pilgrimage yearbook was next to me on the table, and I pulled it closer, furtively glancing around to make sure there were no lingering family members nearby. Mike occasionally liked to bring up Jared to tease me, calling him "Airplane Boy," and I didn't want him to see what I was doing. I anxiously flipped open the yearbook to the page with Jared's message. I felt my heart rate quicken slightly when I saw his handwriting and signature. His screen name—the holy grail, the key to any future communication—nearly shone from the page with a heavenly chorus of angel voices in the background. Gr8tefulDd1023. I clicked open my Buddy List and carefully typed in the name. My breath caught in my throat as I saw the little open door icon appear next to his name, indicating that he was online.

I didn't even hesitate. Just as I had boldly approached Jared in the hostel dining room, I double-clicked on his name to open a new message window.

> **JeSslcA148:** Hey! It's Jessica. You gave me your screen name on the plane home. I just wanted to say hi.

As my words appeared in the chat box and I knew I couldn't grasp them back from the internet ether, I felt my nerves creeping in again as I awaited his reply. *Does he even remember me? What if he met other Jessicas and he doesn't even know who I am?* Another line of text quickly appeared below mine.

> **Gr8tefulDd1023:** Hey! How are ya =)

My anxiety melted away as I read the words, and I was again filled with a renewed sense of promise.

> **JeSslcA148:** I'm good! Writing from our lake house in PA
> **Gr8tefulDd1023:** Sounds nice! I'm just at home in Queens. That sounds better lol

After a few minutes, Jared needed to sign off, but our brief conversation was all I needed. The connection was now made. He was on my Buddy List, and I knew I was probably on his. When we both began our senior year of high school in the coming weeks, and then went on to college after that, we would still be connected. I was relieved to know that the chemistry I had felt with him in Israel had not been extinguished by distance, rather, a door was now open to explore our connection further, albeit virtually.

I knew that Jared probably had a lot of girls from USY on his Buddy List, and he probably sent a lot of smile emoticons. He was flirtatious, and that was part of the reason I was so charmed by him. But meeting him in Israel felt like something significant, and I felt a strong imperative to stay in touch. What I had felt between us—a sort of instant comfort and familiarity, however slight based on our limited interactions—was something I hadn't felt with anyone before. Something deep within me seemed to recognize something deep within him somehow, giving it a knowing look and a slight head nod, acknowledging another of its own kind. I had to know what this was all about, even if we lived in different states and I had no idea when, if ever, we would connect in person again.

CHAPTER TWO

I'll Toast at Your Wedding

I SAT DOWN AT THE SMALL DESK IN MY TINY, shared dorm room at Penn State and opened up my new black Dell laptop. It was 2001, and when I packed for college, I figured I would take out my laptop to use occasionally when I needed a computer. I didn't expect that it would sit in the center of my desk and remain open all the time, utilized as soon as I sat down to my desk, whenever I was in my dorm room. AIM was always open, of course. It was my portal, both to connect with friends at school from my small room at the end of the hallway of my all-girls dormitory, and also to communicate with friends who lived in different places. It was all fair game. When I was signed in I could simultaneously have chat boxes open with my brother Mike back at home, with Leah at school in Delaware, and with the new friend I was about to have dinner with who lived two doors down from me.

I clicked over to AIM now and scanned my Buddy List to see who was online. I clicked the option to set my status to Away. In the field where I could type a custom status message, I paused, debating how much I wished to share with my microcosm of the world today. The bottom section of the small window displaying my status included some of my favorite quotes and song lyrics of the moment, each carefully chosen, even down to the font colors, since I knew that anyone I knew —because *everyone* I knew was on AIM—who clicked on my name would see how I was presenting myself. In painstakingly chosen shades of pink, purple, and orange there were some Dave Matthews Band lyrics, followed by a quote:

"I want to go where I've never been." –Anaïs Nin

Using my favorite wine-colored, unobtrusively styled, and reasonably-sized font, I typed "On the quest for dinner" into the status field, then gave a gentle nod of approval to myself. I hopped out of my desk chair, grabbed my coat and purse, and hurried out of my dorm room to find my friend in the hall and began in earnest said quest.

———

WHEN I RETURNED AN HOUR OR SO LATER, MY stomach full from a cafeteria veggie burger, the taste of the onions I had layered onto my burger from the open buffet still lingering on my tongue, I slung my purse over the back of my desk chair. I hung my coat on one of the high hooks on the side of the wardrobe just inside the door. I moved my finger over my laptop's trackpad to remove the screen saver and was pleased to see that I had several chat windows neatly laid in a diagonal row across the screen, each stacked slightly over the other.

I clicked through the windows one at a time:

"See you in two," from my friend who I had just met for dinner, sent just as I had walked out of my room.

"Yo, are you there?" sent from my brother Mike.

"YESSIE," sent from a friend from high school, Lisa, who also attended Penn State with me, referencing an odd nickname she had given me at one point several years before.

My breath caught in my chest as I clicked to the next window:

Gr8tefulDd1023: Heya =)

Jared. He had moved from New York to Boston, Massachusetts to study at Boston University. He was in no way at the top of my mind as I started my first semester of college; I had far too much on my plate to be preoccupied with the distant possibility of our seeing each other in person again in the foreseeable future. But having someone I had a crush on in my AIM Buddy List who I could flirt with from time to time was a favorite pastime of mine from high school, and I loved knowing that the option was there to do that with Jared. The thought of him seeing the status messages that I posted and knowing my whereabouts warmed me, and I appreciated that I could keep abreast of his. While I truly had no idea whether or not we would ever find ourselves in the same place at the same time again, I wanted to stay in touch to keep the option open that we could connect if we ever did.

Somehow, over the course of the first couple months at school, he had become a bit of a regular AIM Buddy of mine, and we would always chat when we were both at our computers for a decent stretch of time. Our conversations were invariably a bit flirtatious, which was fun. We didn't talk all the time, as we were each busy settling in at school, but it was often enough to be regular, and when we did communicate, it always felt instinctively comfortable. We were both the kind of people who typed the way we talked, so our personalities conveyed over chat in a manner similar to how they would in person. So when we typed to each other, it felt like we were both right there with each other mentally, as though we shared an understanding. And given that I had felt an inexplicable connection to him from the beginning, this meeting-of-the-minds sensation was multiplied about a hundredfold. So when we talked—er, typed—it felt as if we were in the same physical space, slipping away from our dorm room life to meet together in some special exotic locale, on our own unique plane, separate from the rest of the world, in a quiet place where only we understood each other.

The time stamp on Jared's message to me was 6:36 p.m. I glanced at the time in the upper corner of my laptop. *That was from about a half an hour ago.* My eyes darted to my Buddy List, and I was happy to see Gr8tefulDd1023 still signed on. A smile inadvertently spread across my lips as I settled more deeply into my desk chair and began typing into the message box.

> **JeSslcA148:** Hey! What's going on?
> **Gr8tefulDd1023:** Not much, just getting back from hanging out with some of the team. Ate way too much heh
> **JeSslcA148:** Oh what team? Sounds fun
> **Gr8tefulDd1023:** I'm on the BU crew team. It's great. They work us pretty hard but it's a great group of guys and gals.

Gals? Hmmm.

> **JeSslcA148:** That's cool. I don't know much about crew. Ok, I don't know anything about crew
> **Gr8tefulDd1023:** Well we row...in boats.... ;).
> **Gr8tefulDd1023:** It's a fantastic workout. I've been able to bond with the team which has been great being new at school.
> **Gr8tefulDd1023:** I wouldn't have thought I would have time, but a buddy got me to join. Workouts are first thing in the morning so it fits in.
> **JeSslcA148:** That actually sounds nice. I'm always trying to squeeze workouts in where I can.

In truth, I was obsessed with the idea of not gaining the renowned "Freshman Fifteen." I worked out all the time, and the idea of having a built-in schedule to exercise and always having people to work out with was very appealing to me. As I thought more about the idea of being on a sports team at Penn State, something I never would have considered before (isn't that for, like, the real athletes?), Jared's next message abruptly halted my train of thought.

> **Gr8tefulDd1023:** It's been great spending so much time with the women's team also =)
> **Gr8tefulDd1023:** The coxswain, Amy, is actually my girlfriend. I think it's okay that I can say girlfriend now...we've had that conversation heh.

I was stunned. Several thoughts were traveling through my head simultaneously. *What the hell is a coxswain...Girlfriend?! Did I misread his signals somehow? He really seemed single.*

The word "girlfriend" hit me like a gut punch. That special place in the universe where we coexisted when we chatted, independent from everyone else, quietly careened off into the star-studded darkness of deep space. I had thought we shared an understanding, but maybe I had misunderstood. Also, I had never had a boyfriend, so hearing the word "girlfriend" or "boyfriend" bandied about immediately, in my mind, put someone into a class separate and apart from me, in a world that I had yet to understand. This planet was one that was enticing but also scary, mature, and somewhere I just wasn't yet. Jared and I weren't in the same place anymore. And in any case, he was inhabiting his own new and enchanting land with someone else.

My stomach still felt a bit hollow, and I bit back my disappointment as I typed.

> **JeSslcA148:** Wow, that's great! It must be fun
> to train together.

I exhaled deeply. *Oh well.* I held no rights to him. So we had great AIM conversations. I could count on one hand the number of times I had ever seen Jared and spoken to him in person. I had just felt the potential, the hopeful allure of what could someday be if we were in the same place at the same time. It all felt silly in my head now. I willed myself to set aside my feelings for him. *We've never been anything more than friends.* I mustered as much generic, cheery friend energy as I could manage to finish out the conversation before signing offline. *Girlfriend.* I shook my head, still mystified that I had been in such a different place from him.

———

THE FEW REMAINING AUTUMN LEAVES ON the tall campus trees were shades of brown and gold. The rest, which had long since surrendered to the oncoming cold weather and fallen to the ground and dried, crunched under our feet now as I walked slowly in the directly of my dorm with two friends. One was Lisa from my hometown who also attended Penn State, and the other was Kathryn, a new friend who lived on the opposite end of my dorm floor. It was a Thursday evening, and we had all just seen journalist Lisa Ling speak on campus. As we approached my dorm on the corner, Lisa headed across a leaf-speckled grassy area to her own dorm, while Kathryn and I caught the elevator to our shared floor. After the doors parted open with a muted *bing*, I said goodnight and walked down the long hallway toward my room, wondering if I would have any instant messages when I got back. Before I had left that night, I had carefully chosen an away message:

JeSslcA148: Lisa Ling! :D

I always enjoyed posting an intriguing status message to later see who it sparked a conversation with. When I clicked into my laptop now, I felt a warm, tingly flush creep up my cheeks as I saw the most recent IM window holding the front slot above a few others.

Gr8tefulDd1023: Wow! Jealous. Look forward to hearing how that was =)

Jared. We hadn't had much of a conversation since he had dropped the g-bomb a couple weeks prior, but I missed talking to him. Did he miss talking to me?

JeSslcA148: Hey! Long time no talk. Lisa was great!
Gr8tefulDd1023: I like her on The View!

JeSslcA148: Ha...I love that you watch The View.

Gr8tefulDd1023: I like to be in touch with my feminine side =)

Gr8tefulDd1023: That, and it's just a good show.

JeSslcA148: Anyway, what have you been up to tonight?

Gr8tefulDd1023: The usual, just had dinner with a few friends, grabbed ice cream on the way back.

"A few friends". . . a girlfriend?

JeSslcA148: Mmmm, ice cream. What flavor?

Gr8tefulDd1023: Mint chocolate chip. The best kind.

JeSslcA148: The best kind!

Even though it had been several weeks since we had talked, our rapport hadn't missed a beat. *I could enjoy this new "friend" universe. Maybe that's the best place for us anyway. What's the harm?*

Gr8tefulDd1023: So did Lisa say anything interesting?

JeSslcA148: I really liked her. I didn't know a ton about her, I just like The View, but she's really interesting, and has had a lot of cool experiences. She actually had a great quote that I want to remember

Gr8tefulDd1023: Oh yeah?

JeSslcA148: Someone asked her about how she was able to stay informed on so many different topics and she said "I learned to get by, by knowing a little bit about a lot of things."

JeSslcA148: I just thought that was cool.

Gr8tefulDd1023: I like it. Bravo, Lisa.

Gr8tefulDd1023: I agree though. I'd like to know something about everything. Or at least enough to fake it and make everyone think I know everything =)

JeSslcA148: I love that she's been to so many places, and she makes an effort not to travel as a tourist, she really experiences the people and the culture where she goes, and really immerses herself

Gr8tefulDd1023: That's how I want to travel.

JeSslcA148: Agreed

JeSslcA148: Before I went to Israel (the trip where I met you! Ha) I knew that it was going to be a significant trip and I wanted to make sure to truly soak it all in so I wouldn't forget it.

JeSslcA148: And I tried to do that when I was there, I took mental snapshots of everything, sights, smells, etc so it would stay with me

JeSslcA148: I feel like it worked. I can think back and remember everything like I'm there now.

Gr8tefulDd1023: I wish I had done that. It went by too quickly and was a bit of a blur for me.

A blur . . . of making out in the hostel kitchen in the desert?

JeSslcA148: Haha

Gr8tefulDd1023: I guess you were more mature than I was.

Gr8tefulDd1023: Do you want to study abroad?

JeSslcA148: Of course. Probably my last semester, that's what they typically do in my business program.

Gr8tefulDd1023: Business, nice.

JeSslcA148: What are you studying? Do you want to study abroad?

Gr8tefulDd1023: I don't know yet for sure, but probably International Relations. So, yes and yes =)

JeSslcA148: I can't wait to travel again.

Gr8tefulDd1023: Same. It's just the best. Maybe next time I'll take your approach and try and remember it better.

I felt a flush climb my cheeks again, and a couple minutes passed.

Gr8tefulDd1023: So, what are you up to now?

JeSslcA148: Not much, watching Sex and the City. Eating cereal.

Gr8tefulDd1023: Ah, Sex and the City! Good show. Lots of man-ass, though =)

JeSslcA148: Ah, is this part of your feminine side coming out again?

Gr8tefulDd1023: Nice one. Nah, just another good show heh.

Gr8tefulDd1023: Plus, fine, it's an opportunity to see hot women. Well, some of them at least. The one that plays Charlotte - I like seeing her. The others, ehhh.

JeSslcA148: Well that's not nice.

Gr8tefulDd1023: You're right, actually. I don't like to talk about people based on their appearance. It's actually a huge pet peeve of mine if someone calls someone "ugly"

Gr8tefulDd1023: That's not something that a person can control, so it doesn't seem fair to judge them based on that. Plus, it's mean.

I was astonished to hear him say that. I had always felt that way, but so many friends I knew liked to gossip about others, particularly their appearance. It felt like Jared and I were cut from the same cloth.

JeSslcA148: I have always hated when friends talk about someone's appearance. It

is mean. But I like how you put it that way, like
it's something that person can't control.

Oddly deep for a Thursday night. If I had thought that
the revelation of Jared's relationship status meant that we
were going to talk less, I was obviously wrong. We continued talking for several hours. We chatted about everything—our families, our friends, what we liked about our
experiences so far at school, what we didn't. He told me
more about his times with the crew team, making me want
to have similar experiences of my own, in part because it
sounded like a blast, but also so it could be something we
shared. At various moments, I felt exhausted and ready to
close my computer for the night, but the rapport of our
conversation was just too good to end it. There we were,
inhabiting that same space again, that unique plane where
only we existed, in some special realm somewhere between
the center of Pennsylvania where I was and the city of Boston where he was. We were clearly both intrigued by whatever it was that was happening between us because neither
of us could look away, and neither of us could leave and go
to sleep. Maybe because we knew that if we walked away,
if we closed our computers and turned out the lights and
clicked shut the door of that special place, then we might
not see it again. And it was just too intriguing. What was
going to happen next? Who was this person that seemed to
understand me so well?

JeSslcA148: Wow! Is it really almost 1am?

Gr8tefulDd1023: I know, seriously. Time flies when you're having fun.
JeSslcA148: I guess so..
JeSslcA148: You're easy to talk to!
Gr8tefulDd1023: You too. I think we're very similar people.
JeSslcA148: Agreed. That's hard to find.
Gr8tefulDd1023: Agreed.

After a long pause, Jared was the one to message next.

Gr8tefulDd1023: So, bedtime for you?
JeSslcA148: Indeed, I think it is that time. Long week etc etc.
Gr8tefulDd1023: Yeahhh. You've tired me out, yeeesh.
JeSslcA148: Well...we can talk more tomorrow :) It's been really nice chatting.
Gr8tefulDd1023: Indeed. Goodnight, Jessica.
JeSslcA148: Goodnight!

I felt myself glowing as I clicked my laptop shut and heard its fan running, frantically trying to cool down the machine from such heavy, late-night instant messaging. *Wow.* I felt like I had just been on a date. I had never connected with anyone so well, for so long, and about so many things. The instinct about Jared that I had felt before—that our core beings seemed to recognize each other as being of the same kind—was now fully confirmed. There was no doubt that whatever this was that existed between us, whether it was friendship or something more(!), was special. His girlfriend never came up in the entire conversation. *Where even WAS she for all of those hours?*

It felt like it didn't even matter. Our connection felt like an unstoppable force, a given, something that had been written into stone centuries before as part of the great plan of what was to come. It seemed larger than us, so insignificant things like the fact that he had a girlfriend were dwarfed in comparison. Most importantly though, the amount of time he spent talking to me and how he clearly felt comfortable confiding in me made me believe that maybe his relationship wasn't actually all that important to him.

As I laid down to sleep that night, I smiled again, thinking back to our conversation. If before I had felt like I needed to stay in touch with Jared in case we ran into each other again someday, now it felt like seeing each other again was an inevitability. It was just a matter of when. Connections like this were just too rare. And at this point, I was fairly certain that he felt the same.

———

IT WAS SATURDAY MORNING, AND IT TOOK everything I had to pull myself up into a sitting position on my bed. I stretched my arms out to either side and yawned loudly. The night before, I had attended a party with my co-ed business fraternity, at the house owned by the frat. I had recently been making a lot of new friends from the group, male and female, and last night I had deepened some of those connections. But this morning, those new faces were far from my mind; the only thing I cared about was talking to Jared. After our epic watershed talk on Thursday night, the entirety of Friday had passed without us connecting at all. I had started to wonder if he was pulling back because of the obvious elephant in the room: the fact that in spite of our connecting so well, he was currently in a relationship.

I stepped bare-footed onto the cold floor of my dorm room and looked over at the lump in the other bed approximately a yard away from me. My roommate, who I hadn't seen in several days and who often slept in a close friend's room, must have come back in after I had gone to sleep. I reached into the clear plastic bin under my bed, pulled out a large gray hoodie with the words PENN STATE emblazoned in navy across the front, and sauntered the approximately five steps to my tiny desk that backed directly up to my bed.

After pulling on my hoodie and settling into my desk chair, I automatically opened up my email inbox out of habit, and then peered intently at my Buddy List to see if Jared was signed on. He wasn't. I got back out of my seat and took the approximately four steps toward the mini fridge positioned on the floor under our one large window, between my clear plastic shelf unit and my roommate's pink one. As I poured Kellog's Smart Start cereal into a white ceramic bowl from Target, I wondered whether Jared was purposely avoiding me. I added Super Skim Milk from its bright pink carton into the bowl until the flakes were saturated. *Get a grip. He's busy just like you. And taken.* After clicking through some emails and scanning the *New York Times* homepage while shoveling cereal into my mouth with a cheap metal spoon, I gave one last hopeful look toward my Buddy List. No Gr-8tefulDd1023. I sighed, stood up, and grabbed my lavender toiletry caddy from the floor and ambled to the large shared bathroom at the center of the hallway.

I set my caddy down on the narrow metal shelf above the sink and looked at myself in the mirror as I began brushing my teeth. *He is in a relationship. We just connect well as friends. We don't have to talk constantly. He doesn't owe me anything.* I spat into the sink and stuck my toothbrush back into the bin and thought back to our conversation from Thursday night. I exhaled deeply and felt better suddenly. *He was there too. I wasn't the only one in that conversation. We'll talk again. We just need to be at the computer at the same time.*

When my dorm room door swished shut behind me, I set my things down on the floor and immediately glanced at the top right corner of my open laptop that my Buddy List called home. No Gr8tefulDd1023. I couldn't keep doing this all day. I knew I was interested in Jared at this point. I suppose I always was, but just on a new level now, and I had no idea how he felt about me. I couldn't spend any more time hoping we would magically be at our screens at the same moment. I also knew I had to put my mind on something else. I exhaled and sat down at my desk again and clicked on my Buddy List one more time. I scrolled down to the bottom, where all of my buddies that were offline were listed in italics. I scanned through the list and stopped at *Gr8tefulDd1023*. I clicked the cursor on his name to highlight it, then right clicked and saw that there was a list of options, one of which was "Alert." *Something can alert me to when he's online?!* I clicked into the "Alert" option and saw that I was able to select a variety of sounds. I tried them out quietly, all the while glancing over at my roommate's bed to make sure she had not stirred. I clicked onto a sound that played the classic "cha-ching!" of an old cash register and knew that I had found a winner. I double clicked on it, and the alert was set. I smiled, both because I was pleased that I had come up with a way that I wouldn't have to stalk my computer all day, but also because of the sheer humor in the fact that I had selected a sound for Jared signing online that represented how I actually felt when he did. Cha-ching. Jackpot. The only person I'm interested in talking to right now, the reason I'm even sitting at my computer right now and not outside finding something better to do, has arrived.

———

IT WAS AFTERNOON NOW AS I LAY ON MY egg-crate covered twin mattress with my head facing the window. I recrossed my socked feet and continued to stare at the ink-scrawled microeconomics notes in the open notebook in front of me on the bed. I was making an honest effort to study, but the wine coolers I had drank the night before seemed to still be with me, slowly pushing me toward a nap. I leaned my head on my right hand and briefly closed my eyes.

A few minutes later, I was startled by a metallic-sounding noise I didn't recognize. I looked over at my roommate's side of our narrow, rectangular room. *Her cellphone? But that sounded like a cash register . . .* and then I remembered. *Cha-ching.* I jumped up out of bed and ran around the corner to my desk so quickly that I almost skidded in my socks. I moved my cursor to end the screen saver on my laptop and stared at the upper righthand corner of the screen. There it was. Gr8tefulDd1023. Cha-ching indeed. I instinctively glanced at the mirror on the wall to my left and smoothed down my curly hair, which was pulled back into a low ponytail. I rubbed my cheekbones to add some color. *He can't see you.* I sat down on my hard desk chair and stared at the screen. *Am I supposed to message him? Is he going to message me?* I knew that I again needed to put my mind on something else, so I clicked into the New York Times homepage once more and mindlessly scrolled through. Just when I had clicked on a headline that caught my eye, the small rectangle of an instant messenger window appeared on my screen.

Gr8tefulDd1023: Heya

Be cool. I clicked back over to the *Times* article and stared at the words, but my mind was not processing them. I waited a minute or two before clicking back into Jared's message window.

JeSslcA148: Hey there!

Gr8tefulDd1023: How's your Saturday?

JeSslcA148: Good, good. Trying to study.

JeSslcA148: How about you?

Gr8tefulDd1023: Hanging out for a few minutes before running out for a workout. But I wanted to say hello when I saw you on here.

JeSslcA148: Yay! Lucky me.

He was thinking about me too. We talked for only a few minutes, but the fact that Jared reached out to talk to me that day told me everything I needed to know. He was still thinking about our conversation from Thursday night and wanted to stay connected.

Gr8tefulDd1023: I gotta run now, but let's talk later?

JeSslcA148: Sounds good :)

————

I STUFFED MY HANDS INTO THE POCKETS OF my beige and brown plaid fall coat and scrunched my shoulders up toward my ears in an attempt to prevent the bare skin of my neck from being exposed to the sharp, cold breeze. The trees that lined the campus streets were now completely bare, their dark branches stark against a white-gray backdrop of sky. *This coat is not going to get me through the winter.* It was Sunday night, and in each hand I carried a plastic bag of groceries from a tiny market in the student center near my dorm. It suddenly dawned on me that the Jewish holiday of Chanukah was beginning that night. I felt a pang of sadness when I glanced down at the grocery bags in my hands that were filled with granola bars, cereal, and milk; the latter two were my planned dinner. I realized I didn't have any plans to celebrate the holiday.

I thought about Penn State's Hillel, the Jewish student group on campus, and instinctively winced. A few weeks back I had attended an event cold, not knowing anyone, figuring it would be a warm, welcoming, and fun community of like-minded Jews like I had found in USY during high school. The event was a showing of one of my favorite movies, *Keeping the Faith*, along with dinner. I had excitedly burst into the classroom where the event was held and saw a large projector screen in a tiny space with just a small smattering of students scattered throughout. The awkwardness in the air was palpable. Even though I loved that movie, I ended up cutting out soon after it started because the dinner portion was borderline unbearable as I attempted to make conversation with those around me. I thought back to the thousands of students that had attended high holiday services on campus back in the fall. *But everyone comes out of the woodwork for the high holidays.* At the movie showing, though, as I watched Ben Stiller and Jenna Elfman on the screen I remembered thinking, *THIS is Jewish life on campus?!* Maybe there was a Chanukah event happening on campus tonight, but I was pretty sure I wasn't interested in being a part of it. I watched students pass me on either side. *It doesn't even feel like a holiday.*

By the time I got back to my dorm room and set the bags down on my desk, my roommate, as usual, nowhere to be found, I realized I needed to do something, anything. It was Chanukah, and I didn't have a menorah or candles, but I couldn't just go on like it was an ordinary night. I picked up my cordless black landline phone from its upright holder on my desk and dialed the extension for my high school friend Lisa's room.

"Hey Yessie!" she greeted me.

"Hey! Are you around?" I asked in a small voice. "It's Chanukah, and I realized I should do something."

"Oh yeah!" she said. "I just lit a menorah with one of my new Jewish friends from my floor! Why aren't you doing anything?" I was quiet, and so she quickly continued, "Yeah, let's meet up. . . . What do you want to do?"

I looked down at my navy Penn State comfy pants. "Not much. I'm in sweatpants."

"Me too!" she said with a small chuckle. "Meet in the student center?"

I smiled. "Perfect. I'm hungry. I'll bring cereal bars."

Lisa laughed again. "Perfect!"

It was late on a Sunday night, so the student center was deserted, and Lisa and I had each stretched out on our own red metal bench just off a small food court. The tiny grocery store where I had purchased my cereal dinner was around the corner. Next to us was the rear of a bar with round silver trays of pizza slices on top, kept warm under bright orange lights dangling from the ceiling above. I lay on my stomach with my chin resting on my hands, my legs outstretched and crossed behind me. The bench was uncomfortable, and I could feel its metal weave digging into my torso. Lisa lay on her back on the next bench over. She turned her head toward me.

"Are you OK?"

I looked down at the speckled institutional floor below me. "Yeah. It's just been a bit of a shoddy Chanukah." I looked up at her with a small smile. "I'll get over it. Thanks for hanging out with me."

Lisa's eyes lit up and she laughed loudly. "Shoddy? Who says that? Anyway where are those bars you brought? Let's crack 'em open and eat our sorrows away."

I reached under my bench and pulled out the box I had grabbed from a grocery bag just before I left my room. They were a new concoction called Milk N' Cereal Bars made out of actual cereal—in this case, Honey Nut Cheerios—fused together by something resembling a milk-like paste but mostly made of sugar. Lisa looked at the box and appeared even more excited than when I had used the word "shoddy" moments before.

"WHAT are those?!" She tore into the box, pulled out two bars, then handed me one. She ripped hers open and gestured it toward me. "To a shoddy Chanukah!"

I knew I came to the right person to cheer me up. I smiled broadly, tore open my bar, and took a bite.

On my walk back to my dorm room a little while later with a half-eaten box of Milk N' Cereal Bars in hand, I felt warmed from spending time with a good friend, but still somewhat sad knowing the holiday had begun and I wasn't really observing it. When I got into my room, the door swished closed behind me. My roommate was still nowhere to be found. I hung my coat on the hook and glanced at my laptop. I wondered what Jared was up to.

When I signed into AIM, I was pleased to see that he was at his computer.

> **JeSslcA148:** Hey there! Happy Chanukah! :)
> **Gr8tefulDd1023:** Happy Chanukah! =)
> Whatcha up to?
> **JeSslcA148:** Not much...just came back from hanging out with a friend. How bout you?
> **Gr8tefulDd1023:** I'm home for a minute and trying to decide what I want to attend tonight...
> **Gr8tefulDd1023:** There's so many different Chanukah things happening.

I felt a pang of longing and of loneliness—not the first I had felt that night.

> **JeSslcA148:** That's awesome! I wish there was more going on here.
> **Gr8tefulDd1023:** Yeah, it's great. There's actually a group of people outside my window right now singing and dancing.

My heart sank. I wanted to be surrounded by others who were like me, who were celebrating the holiday. I wanted to be where Jared was.

———————

THE LAST SEVERAL WEEKS OF THE SEMESTER went quickly, between finishing up classes and studying for and taking my final exams. I had finally become somewhat honest with myself that I had feelings for Jared. I often listened to the song "Champagne High" by Sister Hazel, which captured my conflicting emotions about liking him but not being able to date him. The song, about the singer attending the wedding of someone he was clearly still in love with, proffered a potential future path for Jared and me if we stayed on our current course. He would continue on with the girl that he was with, and I would be by his side, supporting him as a good friend. One day I would end up at his wedding, purportedly toasting to the new bride and groom while still silently pining for him, wistfully remembering what we had as I watched him walk into the future with someone else.

Still, late at night, while our roommates slept, Jared and I would confide in each other behind the glow of our computer screens. In light of his relationship status, despite my longing, I justified our conversations in my mind as simply two good friends connecting. Still, neither one of us had said anything about being interested in the other. So as far as the record was concerned, we were friends. Plus, it fit more neatly into my mind that way anyway because despite my secret yearning, anything beyond a platonic state represented a fuzzy, frightening terrain locked behind a door, a place I had never been before. What could be behind that door was tantalizing—particularly if Jared held my hand while I stepped over the threshold—but it was still a place I wasn't completely sure I was ready for. So despite how I felt, Jared was simply a friend, albeit one I couldn't wait to get back to my dorm room and talk to, no matter where I was coming from. Even if he was not in a relationship and I was, in theory, ready for one, we had each committed to three-and-a-half more years of study at our respective institutions of higher education that were over four hundred miles apart. What could we ever really be? Despite all of this, I knew that a true and genuine connection with another person, especially one this raw and unveiled, was hard to come by, and apart from whatever we each had going on during our days, I cherished the talks that we had on those nights when we were both online and not yet ready to go to sleep.

CHAPTER THREE

Chasing Daydreams

I SETTLED INTO THE SMALL WOODEN CHAIR at my dorm room desk and slowly opened up my laptop. I glanced out the large window in front of me and saw that a thin layer of ice had formed in the corners of the glass. The winter air outside was bitter cold, and I still felt the chill on my cheeks. I had just arrived back on campus after winter break. My overstuffed pale purple and neon green Adidas duffle bag sat in the middle of the floor by my bed where I had plopped it down minutes before. I rubbed my hands together to generate heat and then pulled the sleeves of my soft, light gray sweater closer to my fingers. My eyes made their way back to my computer screen, and I wondered if Jared was online. We had talked only a handful of times while we were both home for the holidays, and I had been looking forward to the time when we would both be back at our computers on a regular basis again.

I felt my face break into a smile and my cheeks begin to tingle when I glanced at my Buddy List and saw Gr8tefulDd1023 signed on. I took a deep breath and resisted the urge to message him. Within a minute, a message popped up on my screen.

> **Gr8tefulDd1023:** Heya =)
> **JeSslcA148:** Hey there! I just got back to school. How's it going?
> **Gr8tefulDd1023:** Welcome back!
> **JeSslcA148:** Thanks!
> **JeSslcA148:** When did you get back?
> **Gr8tefulDd1023:** Last night. It's good to be here =)
> **JeSslcA148:** Agreed!
> **Gr8tefulDd1023:** Though, it was a little awkward when I almost ran into my ex-girlfriend in the dining hall a little while ago.

. . . Ex-girlfriend?

> **JeSslcA148:** Oh yeah?
> **Gr8tefulDd1023:** Yeah, Amy and I broke up over break.
> **JeSslcA148:** Oh, I'm sorry.
> **Gr8tefulDd1023:** Thanks. It's okay, it was a long time coming.
> **JeSslcA148:** Ahh.

I said "Ahh," but all I could think was, *I knew it!*, with a background choir singing "Hal-le-lu-jah! Hal-le-lu-jah!" in my mind. I exhaled deeply. The path forward was clear. Jared wasn't in a relationship anymore. Nor was I, of course. Our dynamic had not changed. So what did this mean for us moving forward? I didn't know exactly, but I was excited to find out.

> **Gr8tefulDd1023:** I'm headed out to grab some food. Catch ya on here later?
> **JeSslcA148:** Sounds great :)

———

I STRETCHED MY ARMS UP ABOVE MY HEAD with my hands clasped together and stretched slowly to the right and then the left. Then, I shook out my legs and sat down at my desk before clicking on Jared's screen name.

> **JeSslcA148:** Hey!
> **Gr8tefulDd1023:** Heya!

I loved the ease with which Jared and I connected these days. If the seeds of something between us had been planted during the fall semester, nurtured by the light, soil, and water of our late night heart-to-heart IMs, now something green and new had broken through the earth and into the light of day. I strummed my fingers on my keyboard for a moment and marveled over how we talked so frequently now, and how he was such a regular part of my day to day that he had actually begun to influence my life in a meaningful way. It was hard to believe that he had inspired me to join the Penn State crew team and that early morning practices had already begun.

> **JeSslcA148:** So, crew is hard! I'm so sore right now! :-/
> **JeSslcA148:** I like to think I'm in decent shape, but this is kicking my butt.
> **Gr8tefulDd1023:** Yep =) It'll do that.
> **Gr8tefulDd1023:** Good on you for getting started!
> **JeSslcA148:** Thanks :) Definitely still getting used to the pre-sunrise workouts and excessive amounts of push ups while everyone else is still sleeping, and how cold it is on the way to practice... but I like it.
> **JeSslcA148:** Thanks for the inspiration to join!
> **Gr8tefulDd1023:** Anytime. Had a feeling you'd like it, we're usually of the same mind on things =)
> **JeSslcA148:** Indeed ;)

A few minutes passed, and then I saw another message from Jared pop up.

Gr8tefulDd1023: You know, I was telling a buddy about you, and I realized how long it's been since I've actually seen you.

JeSslcA148: A year and a half?

Gr8tefulDd1023: And I realized I don't even have a picture of you since we weren't on the same group in Israel.

JeSslcA148: Ahh, true

I felt my heart start to beat faster. *He was talking about me? He wants a picture of me?* My mind danced with images of Jared and me together: walking on a narrow downtown street hand in hand; sitting in a red booth together with a half-eaten pizza between us; comfortable in a movie theater with his arm around my shoulders. There would be pictures to capture every moment of what we could be. I shook my head and realized I hadn't given him a full reply.

JeSslcA148: Well I can probably find a picture to send you, but only if you send one of you also!

JeSslcA148: Cause I mean...I'm not sure I remember what you look like

JeSslcA148: (kidding. I do. At least I think so)

Gr8tefulDd1023: I think that can be arranged =)

Gr8tefulDd1023: Alas, gotta head to class for now...catch ya later, Jess

JeSslcA148: Later!

I watched Jared's status message go up: "Class," and then I clicked on my own away message box, mulling over what to post. I glanced at the song lyrics at the bottom of my profile, which had changed recently, concurrent with the shift in dynamic between Jared and me this semester. I had added an excerpt from the Dave Matthews band song "Ants Marching," a part about two people looking at each other and speculating what's on the mind of the other but not saying anything. To me that particular line summed up what was going on between Jared and me. By this point something had clearly developed between us, but we were dancing around the subject of admitting that we liked each other. I know we were both wondering what this thing between us was and whether it would go anywhere, but we carefully avoided the topic because there was a risk involved. There was a danger of the other person not feeling exactly the same way, and also of damaging the deep friendship that we had built and come to rely on.

I typed "Out and about" as my away status and then instinctively clicked back onto Jared's name again. I felt my stomach flutter as I noticed that his profile had also changed. He had posted new lyrics from a song called "Chasing Daydreams" by Shades Apart. My brow furrowed as I looked them over—I had never heard of the song or band before. I clicked into my Napster music player and quickly searched for and then downloaded the song.

When I clicked the play button a few minutes later, I heard rhythmic electric guitar picking and then listened carefully when a male voice began to sing. He crooned about going after the person of his dreams and protecting them while knowing that this object of his affection was also there to keep him safe as he fell for them, too. Tiny goosebumps coated my arms, and I felt my face begin to flush as I knew at once that Jared had directed the lyrics in his profile toward me. We were speaking to each other without saying any words.

———

I CLOSED MY SMALL MULTI-SUBJECT SPIRAL-bound notebook, set my pen down next to it on the round table in front of me, and glanced up at the clock on the wall. I had been studying for an hour and a half; it was a good stopping point. I pulled open the door of the quiet dorm study room, crossed the hall, and went right into my room. It was Saturday afternoon, and I was surprised to see that, miraculously, my roommate was inside. She was bustling about, putting the final touches on her outfit before leaving for the rest of the day and night.

"Hey," I said before sitting down at my computer.

I opened up my email and saw that I had a new message from Jared. After our conversation about sharing photos, we had exchanged email addresses, and I had set about searching for a picture I could send to him. Among several that were saved on my computer, I finally found something adequate that I thought I looked good in. It was a shot taken during the trip to Israel where I had met him, a photo of Leah and me at a night market. I was wearing a burgundy seed-beaded necklace that I had just bought at the market that was twisted into two long strands around my neck. My medium-length, dark, curly hair was down around my shoulders, gleaming from the camera flash and set off against the backdrop of the dark night sky.

The subject line of Jared's email read: "Here ya go =)." My eyes darted away from my computer screen and over to my roommate, who was now fumbling around looking for her cell phone.

"I will never, ever in my life be on time . . ." she was saying as she lifted up her pale pink comforter to search her bed.

I glanced back at my screen and anxiously clicked on Jared's email. The body of the message contained only an image attachment. I looked over at my roommate again, who had found her phone and was now cramming it into an already overstuffed tiny handbag with one hand while wrapping a thin bright orange and pink scarf around her neck with the other. I thought for a moment about waiting until she was gone to look at Jared's photo, but I was too eager to see what he had sent, so I clicked on it.

For some reason the photo opened up in a giant size, nearly filling my screen, and was also very closely zoomed in, so I had to scroll to see anything other than the upper left corner of Jared's head. Behind him was an institutional-looking light brown tile background that appeared to be a bathroom or locker room wall. As I continued to eagerly scroll to see his face, I had by now lost track of my roommate, who suddenly appeared behind me.

"Woah! What is that?! WHO is that?!" She cried.

Startled, I quickly glanced over my right shoulder at her. "Oh, um . . . just a friend."

She studied my screen as she smoothed lip gloss from a small round pot onto her lips, first upper and then lower, before smacking them both together. Her face spread into a huge grin. "He's cute!" For a moment she angled her head toward me with raised eyebrows and a knowing look. "Well, I'm off," she said then, and I watched the door to our room close behind her.

Slightly embarrassed, I turned back to my computer screen and resized Jared's photo to an appropriate scale, and then smiled instinctively when his whole appearance came into focus. The large blue-gray eyes, sensitive and mischievous at the same time; the broad smile; the chiseled facial features; the tight, close-cropped curly hair. It was all just as I had remembered.

––––––––

I STARED OUT THE WINDOW OF THE CAMPUS bus, watching the trees pass by against the black sky. It was after midnight, but the neon lights inside the bus shone as brightly as a Walmart in the middle of the day. I had the entire bus to myself. I had just hopped on from a bus stop near Frat Row, a street of Penn State's fraternity houses. The co-ed business fraternity that I was a part of had a house in a different part of campus, worlds away both geographically and conceptually. Tonight I had been to my first true frat party, and I was still cringing from the experience.

Earlier in the night, I had waited in the cold in a long line with several friends from high school outside a large house with Greek letters on it. One of the fraternity members had stood at the top of the steps to the front door, arbitrarily letting a few people in every once in a while, all the while clearly enjoying the power he was able to wield over his fellow students. After a long wait, we had finally managed to be let inside. Upon entering, I had been puzzled as to what all of the fuss had been about. The dark room was dank and smelled of a humid mixture of beer and body odor, and the chunky-heeled black boots I was wearing stuck to the floor when I walked. As I stood with my friends in a small, awkward circle where no one in the room interacted with us, I realized I still felt like I was in high school. I looked around me then and realized I had no desire to be there, pretending this party was cool when it truly felt like nothing of the sort. It felt pretentious, smelly, and gross. At that moment I had a sensation that I was stuck—stuck in that circle, stuck in a group of friends from a past life, and overall stuck in a place where I felt like I wasn't growing as a person. I had quickly said goodbye to my friends, left the house, and caught the bus.

And now, as I exhaled and watched campus go by outside the window on my lone ride back to my dorm, I had a sudden epiphany. *I can't be here anymore. I have to leave.* This was a new realization, but as soon as it hit, it washed over me and left me completely certain. I felt trapped and needed a way out, and I knew there was a path. *I could transfer schools.*

Instantly, dozens of tiny moments added up in my mind—my roommate and I passing like ships in the night and never actually hanging out; the fact that everyone on my floor already seemed to have established groups of friends; how if I wanted to do something fun that wasn't with my business fraternity or new crew people I still didn't know that well, I ended up with friends from high school; the basic truth that I had felt so plugged into Jewish life in the past, but I now had no connection here. The sum total led to one possible conclusion—I had to be somewhere else. To fully be who I was, and in an environment where I could grow into who I wanted to become, I had to be at a different school.

———

ONCE I KNEW I WANTED TO TRANSFER, EV-erything else happened quickly. The morning after the frat party, it took a long phone conversation with my parents before they finally understood that I was serious about my decision and would not change my mind. That same day, I began my applications. I knew I wanted to be at a school in an urban environment, and I soon had a nice list of good East Coast universities. Boston University was on the list. Undoubtedly, it only entered my purview of interest because I knew so much about the school from Jared; his stories about the robust Jewish life there had won me over. Of course, the thought of being in the same physical location as him and what that might mean for our future made it a tempting option, but I tried my best to focus on my own plans and separate him from my decision-making.

Now, it was a Friday night as I sat in my dorm room by myself. I had spent the earlier part of the evening working on some of my transfer applications. I had not told any friends at school that I was applying to transfer, so it often felt as though I was living a double life—during the days, I was training with the crew team and participating as an active member of my business fraternity, all while keeping up with my coursework, but at night, I was secretly setting the stage for the life that lay ahead of me, away from this place.

At this point in the night, I had set aside my applications and was now working on another small project. I had just copied some of my favorite songs onto a blank CD and placed it snugly into a clear case. I reached into the back of my small desk drawer and felt around until I located a narrow pack of colored pencils I suspected to be in there. I pulled them out then grabbed a sheet of computer paper from my printer. I carefully cut a piece of paper to fit the size of the CD case and then drew a large black music note on it in colored pencil before scrawling a title across the top: *Some Good Sound*. I painstakingly filled in the white background with a turquoise pencil. Then, I cut out another square for the inside back cover where I carefully wrote out the artist and song name for each track. On the back, I neatly wrote *To: Jared, From: Jessica*, and then nodded in satisfaction at the finished product. I smiled thinking about how the CD would end up in Jared's hands and he would be able to listen to some of my favorite songs, many of which were meaningful to me because of the connection that I had forged with him.

> **Gr8tefulDd1023:** Hey there!
> **JeSslcA148:** Hey! How's it going?
> **Gr8tefulDd1023:** I got maiiiil today!
> **JeSslcA148:** Oh yeah?
> **Gr8tefulDd1023:** Yep =) I was running around the mail room waving it in the face of everyone I knew saying "I have maiiiiiil!"
> **Gr8tefulDd1023:** I think they were jealous =)
> **JeSslcA148:** Haha, nice.

But did you like it?

I had known that sending Jared the mix CD was a bit of a bold move since we still had not uttered a word about being interested in anything other than a friendship. But I had an instinct to do it, so I did.

> **Gr8tefulDd1023:** But seriously, thank you. That was really thoughtful, and it looks awesome.
> **Gr8tefulDd1023:** Can't wait to spend some time listening to it.

OK. Good.

Gr8tefulDd1023: Be right back...my mom is calling. Ah, she's leaving a message. I'll call her back.

JeSslcA148: Do you talk to your mom often?

Gr8tefulDd1023: Occasionally. She likes to check in with me and make sure I'm not causing too much trouble =)

Gr8tefulDd1023: We have a good chat every couple of weeks.

JeSslcA148: Yeah, I try to talk to my parents every Sunday though I'm not always perfect about it

Gr8tefulDd1023: I like a good phone conversation.

JeSslcA148: Me too.

JeSslcA148: You know, it's funny. We've never talked on the phone before (gasp!)

Gr8tefulDd1023: Really?? Hmpf. I guess that's true.

JeSslcA148: We can remedy that you know...

Gr8tefulDd1023: This is true.

JeSslcA148: Well, let me know when :). I think I could make time.

I was excited about the prospect of talking to Jared on the phone. It felt like something that boyfriends and girlfriends did with each other and was certainly a step up from our regular instant messaging. Also, we hadn't actually spoken to each other since the Israel trip.

While I was keenly curious about what could happen with us, since neither of us had said anything overt yet and because of the physical distance between us, at my core I was protective of myself. I also felt a strong imperative to protect my friendship with Jared, particularly given that I was enmeshed in a moment of transition. I didn't want to let my mind or my emotions get too ahead of themselves, nor did I want to have any expectations. So, I tempered my excitement about what could be possible. *We're just friends.*

My relationship with Jared had layers, kind of like an onion, and neither of us had decided which ones were going to get peeled back to expose the true state of what we were. On the outermost edge, Jared and I were casual friends who had met on a trip to Israel. On another layer closer to the center, we were more regular and continuous friends, ones who didn't see each other often but who regularly checked in on each other's lives. The next layer in was where Jared and I were confidantes, more than just every-once-in-a-while friends; at this stage, at this level deeper within the onion, we were each other's person or at least one of the primary people to whom we would turn when something exciting happened in our lives. This layer was the one that Jared and I shared. When we reached out to each other immediately upon signing into AIM first thing in the morning and late at night, we started and ended our days with each other even though we weren't in the same room. Above all, he was the person I was always most excited to talk with.

The most intriguing part of the onion, though, was the layer beneath the one we currently inhabited. That layer represented the next step, the door that I was so excited about walking through hand in hand with him but that I was also equally frightened by. Beyond that door was uncertainty. Our current layer of the onion was a friendship, albeit a deep and genuine one. That next layer, though, was something else—there were very significant feelings there and likely the beginnings of a concrete, romantic relationship. It felt like we were teetering on the edge of the last layer, dabbling with the idea of whether to peel it back and arrive at that novel and intriguing yet hazy place. But neither of us could do so without the assurance that the other would be there waiting and on the same page.

And now we were going to talk on the phone. Was this a step toward that mystical door, that final level? Jared and I had exchanged numbers, but I knew I didn't have it in me to wonder and wait for when or if he might call me; I knew I was going to call him first. It was just a matter of finding the right moment, which wasn't an easy feat. I didn't have a cell phone yet, only the cordless landline phone on my desk in my dorm room. So, not only did I have to find a time when my roommate definitely wasn't going to be at home, but it also had to be an occasion when I could sufficiently work up the nerve to call. I couldn't have been sitting around for any length of time just waiting to call him because that would give me too much time to think about what I might say and get nervous. Instead, I had to find a time when I would have just gotten back from something else so my mind would be relaxed.

By that Friday, I finally found that ideal combination of circumstances. I had just returned to my room after getting a coffee with a friend from my business fraternity. I had already hung up my winter coat on the hook outside my closet and sat down at my desk. I still had the rest of my mocha with me, so I picked it up and drank the last several sips in one large swig. My body was still slightly chilled from the outside air, so I savored the warmth of the coffee as it went down my throat, the sweetness of the chocolate mixing perfectly with the bitterness of the coffee. I tossed the empty cup into the small metal garbage can under my desk. I rested my left foot on my chair with my knee bent up near my face as I looked straight across the room and out the window at the soft gray winter sky. I set my leg back down on the ground and then picked up the cordless phone. I glanced over at the bright blue square of paper on my desk where I had jotted down Jared's number, then I inhaled and exhaled deeply and quickly dialed the number before I could lose my nerve.

As I heard the phone ring, then ring again, I realized that I had no idea what was going to happen when I heard a voice on the other end. I sighed with relief when I heard the click of an answering machine pick up. My face involuntarily broke into a smile as I heard Jared's voice on the recording. It had been so long since I had heard him speak—since the plane home from Israel. The familiar coziness of his intonations echoed the warmth of the last drops of coffee I had just drank and was equally soothing.

"You've reached Jared Glazer. Sorry I missed you, but leave a message and I'll get back to you soon." *Beeeeeeeep.*

I carried the phone to the window and looked outside as I spoke.

"Hey Jared, it's Jessica . . . I'm calling from Bigler Hall, at the corner of Bigler and Curtin Roads, at The Pennsylvania State University. Just wanted to say hi! Feel free to call back whenever. Talk to you soon."

Click. I sighed as I hung up the phone, content with the message. *Playful, but nice.* The hardest part was done. *Ball, his court.*

———

MY DORM ROOM DOOR SWISHED CLOSED BEhind me as I set down my black leather backpack. I was suddenly face to face with my roommate, who had jumped up from lounging on her bed as soon as she saw me. Her face was white as she looked at me with wide eyes.

"Jess, I think you might have a stalker. Listen to this message I heard someone leave for you." She pointed to the small white answering machine on the windowsill.

I frowned, my coat still on, and walked over to the machine and pressed the messages button.

"Hello, I'm calling for the girl that lives in Bigler Hall, at the corner of Bigler and Curtin Roads, at The Pennsylvania State University. It's Jared . . . sorry I missed you. Give me a call back; look forward to talking. Talk to you then."

Facing away from my roommate, I smiled again to myself at the sound of his voice. I turned around. "Oh, it's fine. That's my friend, Jared. I left him a message saying the same thing, and he just repeated it back to me to be funny."

Her eyes widened again and she exhaled. "OK, phew! I was worried there for a minute that we had to alert the campus police."

I gave a small laugh as I shook my head. "No, no, we're good. Sorry about that!"

I couldn't wait to call him back. Of course, I again had to wait for optimal circumstances, or in the very least, for my roommate to leave.

A little while later when I was alone in the room again, I sat back down in my desk chair and dialed Jared's number. This time, I heard him pick up.

"Hello?"

"Hey, it's Jessica."

"Hey! Glad you caught me."

"Sorry I missed you before." I chuckled. "Your message actually freaked out my roommate. She thought I had a stalker."

"Ahhhh, sorry about that. My bad. That's funny. I don't think I'm your stalker. At least not yet."

I laughed again. "So how's it going?"

I heard the nervousness in my voice as I spoke, and I thought I detected a hint of trepidation from his end as well, masked by humor and bravado. It had been so long since we had last spoken, yet so much had somehow developed during that time. A part of me was apprehensive that talking on the phone would not measure up to the easy dynamic we had chatting online, and I wondered if he feared the same. I tried to regulate my breath to stay calm. *He's just a friend.*

We talked for about thirty minutes before our conversation started to wind down. I had both feet bent up on my chair now, and I wrapped my left arm around my knees to warm my body while I cradled the phone against my ear with my right hand.

"It's cold in here for some reason."

"Aww. I would give you my sweatshirt if I were there."

I felt the temperature rise in my cheeks at the thought of wearing one of Jared's sweatshirts, feeling blanketed in its comfort and security. *I wonder what he smells like.*

"That sounds amazing."

There was a long pause before Jared spoke first. "Well I better run now, I'm supposed to meet a couple friends for dinner."

"No problem. I'm glad we got to talk for a bit."

"Me too."

After we hung up, I remained in my desk chair, processing the conversation. I felt content. Our AIM rapport had definitely translated over the phone, and our call had felt like just another one of our usual flirtatious conversations. It felt like we had taken a positive step forward. We came, we called, we spoke, we hung up, and I felt like we were better for it. I smiled, satisfied that we had taken that step. In the conventional sense, it was the most "real" thing that had happened between us since the plane home from Israel. It added a tangible quality to our now well-developed bond, and also a certain legitimacy, as it confirmed that what happened virtually could happen offline as well.

I opened up my laptop and signed into AIM. I knew Jared wouldn't be there, but there was some crafting I wanted to do to my AIM profile. I pasted in the first few lyrics from the song "Say Goodbye" by the Dave Matthews Band, which generally portrays one passionate night spent between two lovers having an affair before they return to their respective lives, and their friendship, the next day. The first several lines paint a picture of the couple inside together by firelight with a storm raging outside, as they look at each other and understand they want the same thing out of that night. The place referenced in those lines, where the pair was able to seek refuge away from their respective worlds, called to mind for me that unique locale that Jared and I always seemed to inhabit together when we chatted on AIM—our own special land far away from everything and everyone else, where we could be our true selves and each feel completely seen by the other. I felt electric at the thought of sitting alone together in a cabin with Jared, a fire crackling in front of us as we took shelter from the storm. The cabin would be neither here, where I was, nor there, where he was, but in its own place, that neutral land where we could be together. I thought of all of the unspoken feelings between us. The idea of something actually happening—not just physically, but also the beginnings of a real relationship, or at minimum a spoken understanding of how we both felt about each other—was still something of an elusive-seeming dream. However, once we were here in this cabin together, with a storm and the world and life's questions swirling outside around us while we were safe and warm inside, we could finally look one another in the eye and see clearly how the other felt, and know that we were on exactly the same page.

I suddenly frowned as I realized that "Say Goodbye" ends with the lovers resuming their friendship after their one night alone together. Would Jared and I dally with the possibility of romance, only to learn that we were better off as friends? And at that point, would that even be possible?

———————

I LEANED BACK ON MY FOREARMS ON THE wooden dock and looked out at the water, relishing the warmth of the sun on my face. It was spring break. I had made it through the first couple months of crew practices and was now with the team at a rowing camp off of Lake Marion in South Carolina.

I was grateful to have the opportunity to be away from my computer and take a break from talking to Jared and hopefully get some perspective on the situation by creating space. Our days at crew camp were long, grinding, and jam-packed with workouts. This morning's exercises had included squatting against the side of a large garage with weights on top of our thighs. I was relieved to now be relaxing by the lake with some teammates.

As I watched the lake water in front of me shimmer under the hot South Carolina sun, I thought about Jared back at his school in Boston. *It must still be freezing there.* I wondered if he was thinking about me and if he missed seeing me online every day. I sighed and pulled my sunglasses down from the top of my head so they were over my eyes. *But what even are we? Maybe it's good for him to miss me.*

––––––––

A WEEK LATER, I BURST INTO MY DORM ROOM wearing navy blue crew team sweats and tossed my duffel bag onto the floor. I was exhausted from sleeping poorly on the long and loud overnight bus ride back to Penn State. I had my room to myself now, and I couldn't wait to plop onto my bed and make up for lost hours. I shot a quick glance at the closed laptop on my desk. I hadn't looked at a computer screen in a week, and it had felt wonderful. I remembered then that I had told Jared what day I was coming back, and I realized he might be wondering about me. I missed him and was looking forward to catching up, but I knew it would have to be after I slept.

I walked around my desk and sat down in the small wooden chair, then opened up my laptop. I had to press the power button and wait a few minutes for it to turn on this time, and as I watched the screen and waited for it to finish loading, I realized I felt good, refreshed. The distance between Jared and I had felt healthy. As soon as the screen lit up with my familiar desktop of a large, fuchsia-colored tropical flower, I signed into AIM and then quickly typed into the away message field.

JeSslcA148: Back. Tan :) Tired!

The message was one hundred percent directed toward Jared; I didn't even feel like I tried to hide it anymore. Before I could get distracted, I got up from my desk, flopped onto my bed while still in my sweats, and fell into a deep sleep.

When I opened my eyes several hours later, I lay in bed, enjoying the quiet familiarity of my dorm room after the long journey. After a moment, I remembered my computer and wondered if I had a message from Jared. I quickly sat up, stretched, then hopped out of bed and scurried to sit down at my laptop. Sure enough, a message from him had come through minutes after I had posted my away status.

> **Gr8tefulDd1023:** Welcome back! =)
> **Gr8tefulDd1023:** Look forward to when you're back at your computer so we can catch up!

I smiled, knowing that I couldn't have asked for a better message. *He missed me.*

———

IT WAS JUST BEFORE SUNRISE. THE AIR WAS diluted with a foggy haze, and the sky was beginning to turn a milky gray color as the sunlight pressed up against the blackness of the night. I was on a football field: Penn State's field. I heard light crunching sounds beneath my feet as I stepped across the dewy turf. The stadium lights shone brightly from high above me, the cloudy mist in the air swirling visibly in their beams. The field was quiet; there were no players around and no spectators in the stands, so the whole atmosphere was blanketed by a strange and peaceful calm. I walked slowly toward the fifty yard line at the center of the field. *Crunch, crunch, crunch.* There was only one other person in sight. Jared had emerged from the haze and was now walking toward me. *Crunch, crunch, crunch.* I stopped when I reached the fifty yard line, then Jared stood still on the other side of the line, inches away from me. We looked at each other, surrounded by the open expanse of illuminated AstroTurf painted with white lines, shiny from a recent rain, as the perfectly crisp, misty air danced around us. We each took one step closer in, then we were clasping hands. I felt the warmth of Jared's fingers melt through the brisk air around us, and then my lips were touching his.

My eyes jolted open. I looked up at the speckled white dorm room ceiling and instinctively touched my lips, which still tingled from grazing Jared's. I sighed and settled more deeply into my pillow, pulling my comforter tightly around me. *It was just a dream.* I knew intellectually that I had been dreaming, but I also felt like I had actually just seen Jared and that we had kissed, that we had shared an intimate moment away from everyone else in that unusual place. I continued to stare at the ceiling as I tried to process the moment. The kiss had felt so real that I actually felt closer to him now.

The symbolism of the dream was not lost on me, nor was the way in which the events seemed to portend the path that Jared and I were on. In reality, if the two of us were going to take a next step in our relationship and walk through that mystical door into something more, we would likely meet somewhere in the middle geographically. There, we would dance along the line between friendship and something greater. Then there would come a moment when all of a sudden we might take the plunge and cross that line and kiss, and it would become clear that the final layer of the onion had been peeled back to expose the true and final state of what we were.

I had already thought about what it would be like to kiss Jared, mostly in the context of my analytical brain wondering how it would happen, where we would be, who would kiss whom, and what we would say first. In the dream, though, it had just happened. There was no forethought, uncertainty, anxiety, or doubt. The kiss had been so wonderfully simple, so innocent and perfect. I felt my cheeks glowing at the memory. I was excited about the dream, not just because of the embrace, but because it seemed to whisper more broadly of the future, gently directing me to where I was going next in my life after I left Penn State.

There was so much going on for me at this point in the semester. I was still clandestinely making plans to be at a different school that fall, and while I still hadn't confided in anyone at Penn State, Jared knew. As we instant messaged late at night and I told him about the schools I was applying to and kept him informed on my decision-making process, he remained a constant during what otherwise felt like a tumultuous time. And now, the dream felt like an anchor for me. The simple and clear experience with Jared on the quiet football field dissolved all of the noise and uncertainty in my life. The boundary between the present I was living in and the future beyond had been removed, and all that remained was the two of us. I rolled over in bed, my arms hugging my pillow now as I realized that how I felt about Jared was one of the most in-focus things in my life at present.

––––––––––

Gr8tefulDd1023: Heya

JeSslcA148: Hey! How's it going?

Gr8tefulDd1023: Eh, you know. Lots of studying over here. Or thoughts about how I should be studying. You?

JeSslcA148: Same! Can't believe it's already finals time. This semester went so quickly.

Gr8tefulDd1023: Yeah, same. Hard to believe.

Gr8tefulDd1023: So you're headed home for the summer?

JeSslcA148: Yeah for a bit. I need to figure out what's happening next year.

JeSslcA148: You're headed to NY?

Gr8tefulDd1023: Yep. No major plans at the moment.

JeSslcA148: I'm sure I'll make it to NYC at some point. It's been a while and I'm due for a visit.

Gr8tefulDd1023: Yes! Come!

JeSslcA148: Well we'll have to hang out when I'm there.

Gr8tefulDd1023: I'll say it again: Yes! Come!

JeSslcA148: Haha. I will! I'm going to be working at that camp this summer, but not until June.

Gr8tefulDd1023: Ahh right.

IT WAS TRUE. I HAD ALWAYS WANTED TO WORK as a counselor at a sleepaway camp, so I had made plans with Leah to try and do it together this summer. She had slowly fallen out of the process, but I was still excited about the idea; plus I had already invested the time and energy into finding a camp in Madison, Connecticut and applying to and being hired there. So I had decided to press ahead and do it on my own. I had also made these plans before things had picked up so much with Jared; which was all the more reason to make sure we found a way to see each other first.

JeSslcA148: So, if I visited NY, it would be early in the summer.

Gr8tefulDd1023: That works for me. When are you thinking?

JeSslcA148: I'm done pretty early, my last exam is on May 1 and I'm headed home that day.

JeSslcA148: So maybe I could get to New York by the weekend of May 11-12?

I knew that if I saw Jared that weekend, there would still be a couple more weeks after that for things to develop before I had to go away to camp.

Gr8tefulDd1023: Works for me. I'm around =)

JeSslcA148: Awesome!

We solidified our plans. I would come into New York on the bus from Pennsylvania, which was easy to do, and I would stay with my grandfather in Long Island City, Queens. After I spent some time with him, my grandfather would drop me off to meet Jared at his house the next day.

JeSslcA148: I can't wait for the year to be done, and get home, and then get to NY. A change of scenery is what the doctor ordered.

Gr8tefulDd1023: Yeah! Will be great to see ya =)

Gr8tefulDd1023: So I don't want to be presumptuous, but you'll be staying here, right?

My breath caught in my throat. *Staying with him?* I realized I hadn't thought in detail about what would happen when we met up. For me, the most important part of seeing Jared was simply to be in the same room, spending time together. We had been connecting remotely for so many months with something slowly building between us, so it didn't really matter to me where we went or what we did as long as we were together, finally, in the same place. But, I had assumed I would visit with him during the day and stay at my grandfather's at night.

> **JeSslcA148:** Oh! I thought I would stay at my grandfather's the whole time?
>
> **Gr8tefulDd1023:** No way! If you're coming all the way to New York to see me, of course you're staying with me! I couldn't let it be any other way.

Staying over at Jared's house. I hadn't even considered that as an option. Of course he had considered it. The mere idea was spine-tingling. I would get to spend not just the daytime with Jared, but the night also? I still truly had no idea what our visit would entail. Technically, we were still just friends. But the idea of having that much quality time together was not something I wanted to miss.

> **JeSslcA148:** Yeah I mean, that sounds great :) If that's good by you, I'd love that!
>
> **Gr8tefulDd1023:** It's a plan then. You can stay with me Saturday night after we meet up,

and I can make sure you get back to your bus
on Sunday.

JeSslcA148: Sounds great to me.

It sounded more than great to me. By this point in the year I knew that we would find a way to see each other in the immediate future. Still, neither of us had explicitly said "I like you," but in so many ways it felt like we were already in a relationship. And now we had concrete plans. I had set in motion the beginnings of my new life after Penn State.

———

MY DISSATISFACTION WITH MY SURROUND-ings and keeping my transfer a secret eventually weighed on me, and by the time I was taking my final exams, I could not have been more ready to leave campus and go home, then start fresh the next year somewhere new. When I put my pencil down and turned in my last exam, I walked out of the room and left behind the great weight that I had been bearing. I pushed through the glass doors of the academic building and took in a large, deep breath, inhaling the freedom of summer. I practically ran to my dorm to grab my already-packed bags before meeting my mom at her car.

As my mom drove me away from State College, Pennsylvania in our giant gold Ford Expedition, I watched the rolling hills of bucolic farmland dotted with tiny cows and periodic red barns pass by out the window. I felt like I was being rescued from a place from which I had longed to break free. Exhausted from the process of getting to this moment, I sighed deeply and closed my eyes as the highway moved quickly under us. I was finally, literally, on the road to the next step.

CHAPTER FOUR

The Glowing Haze of a Future Unknown

I TURNED OVER RESTLESSLY IN MY CHILDHOOD bed and craned my neck to look at the old brown clock radio on my nightstand. The red digital numbers showed 1:02 a.m. I flipped onto my back again, trying to resettle under my familiar pink and green flowered comforter at my parents' house, then sighed. How was I supposed to sleep when I was leaving for New York to see Jared the next morning? I was only nineteen, but it felt like everything in my life up to this point had essentially led me to this weekend that we had planned together. I hadn't slept a wink yet. I felt completely energized and ready to get on the bus to New York and begin my weekend with him.

I eventually managed some small spurts of sleep over the course of the night before, at last, the morning arrived. I felt deeply groggy when I finally switched off my alarm after several snoozes, but I pulled myself out of bed, grateful to know that I had two hours of bus time ahead of me that I could use for catch-up sleep.

"JESS!!" my mom yelled up the stairs.

I had slept in later than planned, and I knew she was concerned now that I was going to miss my bus.

Fortunately I had already picked out my clothes the night before and my bag for the weekend was packed, so it wasn't too long before we sat in the car together on the way to the Scranton, Pennsylvania bus station. My mom looked over at me as the car slowed to a stop at a red light.

"So who is this friend that you are going to see? Is it someone that you're interested in as more than a friend?"

I tried my best not to react or display any emotion. "He's just a friend that I know from USY, and he was nice enough to let me stay with him while I'm in the city."

I looked out the window, trying to stay nonchalant as the car turned left. I knew that Jared was certainly more than that to me, but that was not something I had said out loud to anyone yet.

———

I SLEPT MOST OF THE BUS RIDE TO NEW YORK, carefully leaning the side of my cheek onto my hand so as to not disturb my curly hair by mashing it against the bus seat behind me. My eyes opened just as we were pulling up to the Lincoln Tunnel that would lead us into the city. The tunnel had always been an important demarcation line on my childhood trips to New York; after we passed through its dark enclave lined with tiny rows of lights and emerged into the bright daylight on the other end, we had officially arrived. I felt a small flutter in my stomach as we inched closer in the traffic. Then, as I began to process how close we were to disembarkation, I felt a brief sense of panic. Realizing the effect my sleep had on the inside of my mouth, I quickly dug into my camel-colored leather tote bag and felt around until I unearthed a pack of gum. *Thank goodness.* I unwrapped a small slice and popped it in my mouth.

It was always exciting to go to the city, but this time, I was going to see Jared. This magnificent place was going to be the longitude and latitude where we would actually connect in person and where questions about the two of us that had been open for so long might finally be answered. I spit my gum back into its foil wrapper before balling it up and tossing it into the small black trash bag tied to the empty seat beside me. I reached back into my tote bag and pulled out a round compact and a tube of neutral mauve lipstick. I scanned over my face in the reflection and then quickly smoothed a fresh coat over my lips before clicking the compact shut. Overall, I felt confident. As the bus slowly made its way into Manhattan, I felt as though I was exactly where I was supposed to be in this moment, on my way into New York to see Jared. It felt so completely right. All of the things and people and circumstances in my life the prior year had led me to this particular moment, and I was ready.

Then, in one instant, a sudden fear of the unknown began to creep inside my body, slowly encapsulating me.

Will this be awkward? What if it isn't like it is online? Then I thought of a line from the Dave Matthews Band song, "#41," about making your own way into and out of a situation. I took a deep breath and digested the meaning of the words, and they calmed me down, paving the apprehension over with reassurance. I would walk confidently into this situation that was truly unknown and unlike anything I had done before, one that I was completely emotionally invested in. I had set this thing in motion, and it was happening just as I wanted it to. And now it was up to me what happened next.

————

SOON, I SAT AT THE DESK IN THE SPARE ROOM used as an office in my grandfather's apartment in Long Island City, Queens. It was Friday night, and I had plans to stay here before meeting up with Jared the next day. The desk was pushed right up against a large window, and as I gazed outside at the dark night, savoring the vantage point of Manhattan just across the East River, I felt truly enveloped by the city's bustling embrace. I watched the tiny headlights shining from cars as they streamed down the highway along the water, and the bright and varied sparkles of light from the motley of tall buildings all beckoned possibility. It was all so close that I felt like if I reached through the glass, I would be able to touch the facade of a tower and be electrified by the riveting and unrelenting voltage of Manhattan such that I, too, would become a part of its radiant landscape.

As the city lights continued to dance against the dark sky, their movement began to mimic the bubbles of excitement rising in my stomach as I thought about how I would be seeing Jared the next morning. Soon the radiant flecks began to blur together into a glowing haze, the dazzling fog of a future unknown.

I blinked and shook my head, pulled back to reality as I looked down at the white landline phone on the desk in front of me. I had come into the office so that I could call Jared to confirm our plans for the next day. After reaching down onto the floor for my leather tote, I pulled out a small purple notebook where I had scrawled his home number. My cheeks flushed slightly when I flipped it open and saw his name next to the numbers jotted in blue ink. I picked up the receiver and took a deep breath as I slowly dialed.

"Hello?"

"Hey, Jared? It's Jessica."

"Hey! Are you here?"

"I am! I got in a couple hours ago, and I'm at my grand-father's apartment now."

"Great! Long Island City, right?"

"Yep!"

I felt elated hearing his voice, knowing that we were so physically close to each other now. Everything was as it should be. I confirmed his address for the next morning, and we agreed on a time to meet.

"So, see you tomorrow then!" I said excitedly.

"Can't wait," Jared replied heartily before we hung up the phone.

Neither could I.

———

THE NEXT MORNING, I SAT IN THE CUSHY, off-white leather front seat of my grandfather's beige Cadillac as we drove through the tight streets of Queens. I looked down at my carefully chosen outfit of tight, dark blue Gap jeans and a wine-colored long-sleeve V-neck shirt with a pattern of subtle sparkly gold dots starting from the bottom and gradually fading toward the top. I picked up the silver teardrop-shaped charm around my neck—my favorite necklace, one I had bought at the Tiffany's flagship store on Fifth Avenue the last time I was in New York. It was the first thing I ever owned from Tiffany's, and I had felt very adult making the purchase. I moved the charm around gently in my hands now as I watched the rows of houses pass by outside the window. I couldn't believe I was about to see the place where Jared grew up. And he would be actually, physically standing there to greet me, a truth that still felt surreal.

His neighborhood was very different from the rolling hills of Pennsylvania where I grew up. The houses were neatly packed in a row on the street, all resembling one another in style, each with a set of concrete steps leading up to the front door. We slowly pulled to a stop at the curb outside the house with the street number that Jared had given me. The front door opened just as we parked, and there was Jared. He stood and waved, his attractive build, cropped short curly hair, genuine smile, and kind eyes were all exactly the same as when I had noticed him across the room in the desert in Israel. My grandfather gave an approving smile and nod before I said goodbye and got out of the car.

Jared came outside to help me lug my small duffle bag up the stairs as I turned to wave to my grandfather once more. We made our way inside the door, and Jared set my bag off to the side before looking directly at me with his arms extended out, a huge smile spread across his face.

"Hi!" he said warmly.

As we shared a quick hug, I felt a slight nervousness, reflected in what I thought I detected as his own.

"Welcome to my humble home! Can I show you around?"

He led me through the house, briefly introducing me to his mother in the kitchen. At first I was surprised to see her, since Jared hadn't mentioned anything about her leading up to our trip. *Well, she does live here.* We chatted very briefly before Jared walked me upstairs. There were so many things I wanted to say to him, but I knew we would have plenty of time to be alone together. Once upstairs, we stopped outside his childhood bedroom.

"This is where I'll sleep. You'll sleep on the couch downstairs, if that's cool. Mom's rules."

I felt myself blush slightly. "Of course!"

I peered into his room for just a moment. It was small with a twin bed pushed against one wall under a window. The walls were covered with white wallpaper with tiny blue stars all over it that I loved. I instantly pictured Jared in here as a young boy, small and curious with wildly curly hair, lying in bed and looking up at the stars on his wall, the noises of the city audible from the street below.

"What?" Jared asked as he noticed me quietly looking into his room. "Want to see the rest of the house?"

I snapped out of my daydream. "Oh nothing, I just like the wallpaper," I said quickly, then smiled. "Sure, let's go."

We ended up in a room that looked like an office with tall CD towers lining either side of a desk. I spotted the familiar red cover of the soundtrack from the musical *RENT*.

"Ooo, *RENT!*" I said excitedly.

Jared grinned. "Should we listen?"

I nodded vigorously. "The answer to the question of whether we should listen to *RENT* is always yes."

We sat down in two chairs in front of the desk as Jared popped the disc into the CD drive on the computer.

"I love 'Light My Candle,'" I told him. "I actually sang it as a duet with a guy from my Israel Pilgrimage trip during our talent show on the last night."

I thought back to that night on the stage at our hostel in Jerusalem when I had looked out at the sea of those sixty-some faces, most of whom six weeks prior had been complete strangers to me but with whom I now shared so many memories, and whose faces I knew I would miss when we all returned home to our real lives the next day.

Singing "Light My Candle" dressed as the character Mimi, in a borrowed red mini skirt and black fishnet stockings, had been the capstone to a transformational summer.

"Wellll, then let's have at it," Jared said with a smile.

I heard the pop-y opening notes of the song play from the computer's speakers, then Jared confidently sang out the opening line of the male character, Roger. I smiled as I sang Mimi's line right after him. As we sang back and forth in time, I looked at Jared and almost couldn't believe that we were sitting here together, after all this time, and with so much lead-up. I felt deeply happy tying together my personal significance for "Light My Candle" to this important moment with him. He was the only person I wanted to sing a duet with, real or metaphorical. While we continued belting out the words, I glanced down and noticed that although Jared and I were already sitting on chairs close to one another, he had put one of his feet on the lower bar of mine, so that our legs were now even closer together.

He smiled broadly again as the song ended. "I didn't know you could sing."

I shrugged. "Well, I *like* to sing."

———

JARED DID NOT LIVE FAR FROM THE SUBWAY, so we made a plan to take the train into Manhattan to spend the day there. As we gathered our things to leave, a landline phone rang from a small wooden table in his family room. After a few rings, Jared finally decided to answer.

"Hello? Oh, hey. Yeah. Yeah. Sure. So I actually have a friend visiting right now, but can I call you tomorrow? OK cool. Will do. Yeah. Yeah. See ya." He set the phone back on its cradle. "That was Rachel, a friend from school," he said flatly. "Obviously it's not a good time."

I wasn't surprised that a girl was calling him. Jared was an exceedingly charming person, not to mention a tremendous flirt, and I would have been shocked if he didn't have female admirers back at school. I didn't feel threatened, though. I knew that Jared and I had a special bond. Plus, he was clearly deferring to me. I picked up my tote bag and stood up.

"Oh, no problem. Ready?" I noticed something in Jared's hand. "What book is that?"

He turned it over. "Oh, *The Poisonwood Bible*. It's one of my favorites. I always like to have a book with me when I'm out, just in case I end up with a moment to read on the subway or something."

I smiled. "I like that. But you'll be able to talk to me on the subway this time, right?"

Jared grinned back sheepishly. "True. Habit, I guess. Have you read this?"

I shook my head, and then he held the book out to me. Its tan cover was worn on the spine and the corners on the front cover were folded back from use.

"Here, borrow it."

I looked it over in my hands. "Oh cool, thanks!"

I gingerly tucked it into my bag and loved knowing that I would be bringing a piece of the weekend back home with me.

A little while later, we walked side by side along the Manhattan streets, making our way to Central Park. I quickly caught our reflection in the shiny facade of a building beside us. After giving myself a speedy once over, I felt ebullient at the sight of the two of us strolling together like a couple.

We periodically snuck glances at one another as we chatted excitedly. Jared was as handsome as I had remembered, and I was still immensely attracted to him, even more so since I had gotten to know him so well over the past year. A few times our hands nearly grazed each other's as we walked, and it felt like we should hold hands. I certainly wanted to, but neither of us had taken any clear steps across the friend line yet.

We eventually arrived at Central Park and wandered together around the tree-lined paths as we continued to talk. We stopped when we came upon an area with a few large rocks that looked like a nice place to sit. It felt as though we were both eager to have an opportunity to sit and be close to one another, to really look at each other, which would feel like a reward for the last year of connecting online with so much anticipation.

As we settled in together on the smooth gray surface of a boulder, Jared said, "You know, I was telling some buddies about who was coming to visit me this weekend, so I was describing you. I said, 'You're awesome and basically just like me but in female form.'"

I smiled, and he continued, "Then I realized that sounded kind of cocky because that's like saying 'I'm awesome.'"

I laughed. *He told his friends about me.*

"Well, thanks," I said.

I felt utterly content sitting next to him as we talked and took in the afternoon sun.

"Oh, I brought some photos to show you," I said, and pulled out an envelope that I had prepared with some carefully selected shots.

Despite how much we had connected recently, Jared still didn't know what any of my friends or family looked like, and I wanted him to know everything about me. He flipped through the small stack of pictures as I described the faces in each one. He stopped and lingered on a photo from my junior prom with me in the center and a friend on either side of me. I was wearing a bright coral strapless dress with a layer of tulle beneath the skirt that made it pouf out just enough to create a princess aura. My hair was smoothed back into an updo.

"You look beautiful," he said. "You are clearly the most beautiful girl in that photo."

His comment made me slightly uncomfortable, but I knew it was intended as a compliment, so I gave a small smile back. Then he turned and fixed his steely blue gaze squarely on me.

"You are beautiful."

The corners of my lips turned up again, and I looked away shyly this time as I felt myself blush.

After a while, we got up from the rocks and left the park to cross the street to the Museum of Natural History. We climbed the vast concrete steps of the stately building with its grand columns lining the front, and soon we were meandering through dimly lit corridors with illuminated displays about space. We occasionally stopped to look into a glass case, but we were exponentially more focused on our conversation and on simply being together than on any of the exhibits.

We eventually located a nearby elevator bank to head upstairs, and before long, the shiny metal doors split open to reveal a crowd of people. We shuffled in and squeezed to find space next to each other in a front corner. I felt my heart beat faster as we were pressed close to each other amidst the crowd. As the hefty elevator slid slowly in an upward direction, Jared, just inches from me, gestured to the tiny silver hoop earring in the upper cartilage of my left earlobe.

"I like that," he said.

I reached up to touch the narrow silver band. "Oh, thanks! I actually got it done in Israel."

Jared raised his eyebrows, looking simultaneously bemused and impressed. "Wow, I thought they were pretty strict about piercings on those trips, no?"

I shrugged. "They are. But the staff liked me, and I didn't do it until a few days before going home. I hid it behind my hair until we left."

"Nice," Jared said with approval.

"There were several of us who managed piercings on the trip without getting caught," I continued. "A tongue piercing and another ear piercing, and we all got a picture together on the last day."

Jared raised his eyebrows again, this time with some skepticism. "You mean to tell me someone hid a tongue piercing? That's just impressive."

I nodded slowly and touched the tiny hoop again. I loved how it always reminded me of that formative summer. Standing so close to Jared now, who I had met on that same trip, while telling him about the experience made it feel like I had come full circle from one defining moment to another, now interconnected.

Before long we were on the subway headed back to Queens. My legs felt tired from all of the walking we had done, and I was grateful to have found a seat. Jared stood directly above me, holding onto the metal handle hanging from the ceiling. As he held on and looked down at me, his arms were flexed, showcasing his large and noticeably toned muscles, etched with definition from a year of rowing crew. I tried not to visibly blush.

As the train lurched forward into the darkness of a tunnel, I caught a brief glimpse of my hands in my lap, illuminated by the bright lights inside our subway car. I touched my fingers together. *This is real.* So much of the day had felt unreal, almost unbelievable, to finally be in person with Jared. Most of my relationship and dynamic with him thus far had been virtual, impalpable, and essentially in my mind. Looking down at my hands now briefly grounded me and reminded me of the tangible quality of what was happening as my back leaned against a pale blue subway bench and Jared casually stood over me as we rode toward his home.

We climbed the steep steps out of the underground and emerged into the light on the sidewalk above. I suddenly felt a dull churning in my stomach, and realized that I had been so exhilarated roaming the city with Jared that I had forgotten to eat. I turned to him.

"Do you mind if we grab some food real quick?"

He shook his head. "Sure." He gestured toward a street cart just outside the subway exit. "How 'bout this?"

I frowned slightly as I studied the unimpressive-looking cart. *Well not exactly what I had in mind.* I had pictured us sitting down together at a small table in a restaurant on a proper date. But I couldn't say that. And I was so hungry that I heard my stomach audibly rumbling now. I gave a small shrug.

"Sure, works for me."

We approached the cart, and I scanned the laminated menu on the outside. I only ate meat that was kosher, which left me with exactly one choice—a large, greasy, garlicky rolled breadstick. I wasn't particularly excited to consume that, but I didn't know how long it would be before I had a chance to eat again, so I reluctantly told the vendor I would like one. I went to pull my wallet out of my tote bag.

"I got this," Jared said.

I shook my head, "Oh I don't mind."

But Jared insisted. "You came to visit me. It's the least I can do."

Before long, I held a shiny breadstick wrapped in red and white checkerboard-print wax paper. I inspected it suspiciously and waited until Jared also had one in his hand before taking a bite, then in spite of myself, I quickly ate the entire thing. It felt heavy in my stomach, and I immediately felt its grease on my skin. But at least I wasn't hungry anymore. Jared ate his entire breadstick as well.

As we walked back to his house, the atmosphere around us began to gray as the sun embarked on its nightly descent.

"It's getting dark out," Jared said. "Can I take you to one more place today?"

I thought with hope that maybe we would finally have the romantic moment I was seeking.

"Of course," I said, and he smiled.

"Great. If we hop in the car, there's a bridge I want to take you to see that looks beautiful lit up at night."

Now thaaaat's what I'm talking about.

"Yeah, that sounds great."

A short while later, Jared's car pulled into a small, quiet parking area by some water. By now the sun had completely set and the sky was black. Just ahead of us I could see a large bridge running across the water, bedecked with bright lights that twinkled a shimmering reflection into the river below.

"We're here," Jared said as he shifted the car into park. "The Throgs Neck Bridge at night."

I gazed out the window again. "It's so pretty."

Jared clicked his seatbelt off and reached for his door handle. "Out here is the best view, though."

I felt a simmer of excitement start to build in my chest. *OK. This is where something happens.* After we climbed out of the car, Jared led me to a bank of large, dark rocks that stretched out into the water, forming a natural pier.

The rocks, only sporadically illuminated by the lights from the bridge, blended into the opaque water on either side. I stepped carefully, unsure which of them might be slippery in the dark night. Jared was a few steps ahead of me, and I wondered why he wasn't waiting for me, why he didn't take my hand. We were alone outside with a scene of beauty in front of us; all of the ingredients were present for a truly romantic moment. And we were finally together after all this time. *Maybe there aren't any additional layers to the onion. Maybe we are just friends.*

I eventually reached Jared where he had stopped further out on the rock pier, and now we stood gazing out at the bridge together, watching its lights twinkling like stars against the inky black sky. We were close together but not touching. *OK, this is romantic.* I stood silently, waiting, certain that Jared would make a move to kiss me. I snuck a quick glance at him and saw that he simply seemed taken by the view of the bridge and wasn't looking at me at all. I turned back to face forward again and took a deep breath, trying to imprint into my memory the image before me, this moment with Jared, this whole unbelievable day. *Take it all in.* Out of the corner of my eye I could see that he was looking at me now. *Be cool. He's going to kiss you. Don't panic. Just keep looking at the bridge . . . yeah, the bridge.*

A few long minutes went by. There was complete silence between us, dotted with an occasional murmur of "Wow, it's so pretty," or "I love all the lights." Then all of a sudden Jared seemed to snap back to life.

"OK, want to head back? It's getting cold!"

His words sliced through the air that moments before had been ripe with promise. I was jolted back to reality now, too, and became instantly aware of the cooler breeze against my skin. The image of Jared kissing me on that rock pier and solidifying our identity as something greater than friends quickly dissipated into the dark water below us, rippling away on the light waves and into the night. *Friends indeed.* All at once I felt embarrassed that I had even entertained the idea that something different was going to happen. I also felt slightly annoyed. *Why bring me to such a romantic spot if you didn't intend to make a move?* I couldn't let him know how I felt, though, because I had never indicated that we were more than friends, either. We stepped back across the rocks toward his car.

I clicked my seatbelt into place then looked out the window and sighed, unsure what I should say to Jared next. Just as he was about to turn his key into the ignition, he suddenly pulled his hand away.

"Actually, I just want to take one more quick look." He opened his car door and stepped back outside, holding the door open as he gazed back out at the bridge for a few more seconds.

Wow, maybe he's trying to imprint the memory also.

I felt my annoyance subside slightly. After a minute, Jared was back in the driver's seat. As soon as he closed his door, I was hit with an unmistakable whiff—a fart. I thought back to the greasy street cart breadsticks that we had scarfed down for dinner. I turned toward my window and suppressed a chuckle as I simultaneously tried not to breathe in the contaminated air. I shook my head slightly, marveling at how Jared hadn't really wanted to get one more glimpse of the bridge; he just really had to fart and had made up an excuse to get back outside so he could *let 'er rip* and then slip back into the car, transgression unnoticed. But his plan had not worked effectively since he didn't stay out long enough to let the smell subside and instead carried it back into the car with him. As we pulled out of the parking lot, I felt slightly embarrassed for him as I continued to work to avoid the smell that I could not escape but also could not acknowledge.

Now I felt somewhat deflated. First, he lured me somewhere beautiful and then showed no interest in anything romantic. Then, I'm subjected to a fart in close quarters. I wasn't sure what I expected, but for some reason it didn't feel right to me that he had made up a reason to get back out of the car. Certainly full honestly would not have been appropriate—"I really have to let loose something serious right now, those breadsticks are *not* sitting well. Do you mind if I step outside the car for a second then linger long enough for the smell to pass so I don't have to subject you to it when I return?" Maybe the right answer would have been not to fart at all, to the degree that was possible. If he had stayed in the car but couldn't hold it in and ended up cutting one anyway, we would probably have had to acknowledge it. That would have been somewhat embarrassing for him, but I would have found it hilarious. It might have even brought us closer together to suddenly inject that level of comfort into our relationship. But instead, I now just felt awkwardly forced to pretend it didn't happen.

Soon we arrived back at Jared's house, and I was still somewhat flummoxed about the state of our relationship but had gotten over the fart as the ride home had allowed the air to literally and proverbially clear. We settled onto the couch that I was going to be sleeping on in the family room.

"So, should we watch a movie?" he asked.

I now had no idea what to make of the evening and felt as though I was simply along for the ride, waiting for him to let me know where we were going to stop. But I was grateful to be inside and warm on the couch.

"Yes, that sounds perfect."

We climbed off the couch to scan through the DVD collection in the glass-doored cabinet to the right of the TV.

"*Memento* is always a good choice," he said, pointing to one.

I picked up the case and turned it over. "Oh, really? I haven't seen this."

Jared looked at me with surprise. "You haven't seen *Memento*?! It's settled then."

We planted ourselves on the beige carpet and leaned our backs against the couch to have a close, square view of the TV. Jared put the DVD in then hit pause and stood up.

"Do you want some wine?"

Of course. That's it. I finally understood what was going on. Since there was still ambiguity between us, of course he would want to add alcohol to the mix to more easily allow for the possibility of edging beyond the friend zone.

"Sure, I'd love some."

As Jared disappeared into the kitchen, I briefly wondered whether his mom was still at home somewhere, then I frowned and shrugged to myself. He didn't seem to have any qualms about busting open a bottle, and I was following his lead here, so neither did I.

I waited on the floor, leaning against the couch with my knees bent while the home screen for *Memento* displayed on the TV. I glanced down at the tiny burgundy flowers dotting my olive green socks then looked back up at the doorway toward the kitchen where Jared was pouring us wine. It felt like the atmosphere had shifted. *Now things are going to get interesting.*

Jared returned to the room with two short, clear juice glasses, each filled about halfway with a light red wine. He handed me mine then sat down to my right. We each took a sip before setting our glasses down on the floor in between us, then he pressed play on the movie. I glimpsed Jared out of the corner of my eye. It was still hard to believe that we were here, sitting side by side with approximately two juice glasses' worth of space between us, when before today we had not been in the same room together in two years. And at least for the last six months, that was all that I had wanted. We were next to each other now, but not touching. No one had crossed that line yet.

We watched the entire movie. I still hadn't had much to eat all day, so I took only very small sips from my wine. I looked over to see that Jared's was nearly gone.

"Want to see what's on TV?" he asked.

I nodded, and he clicked the remote, eventually selecting the movie *Zoolander*. Before settling back in against the couch, he carefully moved both wine glasses to his right, and I felt my heart flutter as he sat down slightly closer to me. The literal and metaphorical line had narrowed.

A few minutes into the movie, Jared shook his head and said, "OK, this is a weird movie, right?"

I laughed, grateful to break up some of the unmistakable tension in the room. "I know! I have no idea what's happening right now."

Maybe neither of us could engage with the movie because it was so lighthearted while what was happening off-screen with us felt so serious, so important. We started making fun of what we saw on the TV.

"OK seriously, WHAT is going on?!" I asked as we watched Starbucks drinks fly from a gas station explosion.

Then I realized that neither of us was really even watching the movie anymore, we were only pretending to do so. Jared slid closer to me then positioned himself a little bit behind me, so that I leaned against him, resting on his chest.

"Is this OK?" he whispered.

Trying to sound as cool as possible, I managed a small, "Yeah."

I felt my breathing speed up with nervousness, and I took some deep breaths to regulate it so he couldn't sense how I felt. Suddenly, I was startled as I felt the quick *pound pound pound* of his heart beating directly beneath where my head lay against his chest. *He's nervous too. OK, be cool.*

Keep watching Zoolander. *What the HELL is this movie about?* And then I felt Jared's hand gently on my chin as he turned my face toward his. Slightly surprised, I looked up at him, and then there were his lips on mine. For a second, I felt the gentle tip of his tongue on my own as he parted my surprised lips just slightly. And then he wrapped his arms around me from behind and gave me a quick squeeze.

We had kissed. It was so swift and simple, but it felt momentous. The line between a close friendship and something more, something romantic, that demarcation between the outer layers of the onion and the innermost sacrosanct tier, had officially been crossed, leapt over by us both with the tiniest of kisses. The middle of the football field, the fifty yard line between us had evaporated into a thin mist now, ultimately dissolving completely into the gray sky around us. I leaned back against Jared's chest, and we sat together in a comfortable silence. The air in the room had changed palpably. Jared and I had kissed.

Sitting in his arms, I felt equal parts deep contentment and giddy excitement. This new beginning with him felt like a microcosm of where I was at in my life. I had just left one college behind and was about to start at another in the fall, and soon I was going to plunge into a new experience working at a sleepaway camp in an unfamiliar place. As I had perceived the night before when I gazed out my grandfather's window at the spectacular lights of Manhattan, I again felt bathed in the notion that the world was open in front of me, and the path toward who I was to become was increasingly apparent. It didn't even matter what happened next—with the rest of this weekend, between Jared and me, or with my next major-life steps, because at this moment, everything felt luminously clear.

———————

I WOKE UP WHEN JARED JUMPED ONTO THE couch where I slept.

"You awake?? How'd you sleep?"

I was lying on my stomach, so I turned up my head slightly and squinted one eye open without fully leaving the pillow. Jared was sitting on the couch near my head, his legs crossed under him and a huge smile on his face.

"Gooooood," I grumbled. "Still kind of sleeping. Ah-hhh!" I shouted then, startled by Jared who had now playfully climbed over and lay facedown on top of my back. "OK, OK, I'm awake," I said begrudgingly, trying to push him off as I sat up. I yawned, conscious that I likely had morning breath. I pulled my hair back with a black elastic from around my wrist.

Jared had now thankfully relocated further away onto the other part of the couch. I saw that he was still in his sleep clothes: a pair of gym shorts and a white T-shirt with the sleeves cut off, which emphasized the muscles in his upper arms. The shirt had a navy blue circular logo with the words "Camp Moshava" and some Hebrew letters written on it.

I looked at Jared as I rubbed the sleep from my face and saw raw tenderness in the gray-blue oceans of his eyes as he gazed back at me, his smile sincere. In that moment, I abruptly saw everything that he was—his vulnerability, his boyish earnestness, his deep caring for me. He seemed so unguarded, as though his entire being were in front of me. All at once, I felt terrified. *I am not ready for this.* I averted my eyes and looked down at my nails. Like a bolt of lightning straight to my core, Jared's sense of comfort and intimacy all of a sudden seemed like too much. It made me feel tethered and defined at a time when all I wanted in my life was for a world of possibilities to be open to me. My stomach sank slowly and a heaviness engulfed my chest now as the air instantly felt thinner, as though he was taking some of what I needed to breathe on my own.

We had spent the last year slowly climbing a hill as we made our way closer to a twinkling city at the top that glimmered with opportunity and potential. But now we had arrived in that seemingly mystical and mysterious place; we had opened the door, walked through, and we were here together now, but for some reason I didn't like the view. It all felt wrong, and I didn't know why. It was as though all of the butterflies that had been milling around in my stomach for the last year had somehow escaped and fluttered off into the bright blue New York spring sky, and a dull apprehension had now settled into their former habitat. And now, all I wanted was for Jared to go back upstairs and put a real shirt on and not be in his sleep clothes anymore because maybe we shouldn't be quite so comfortable together. For in one instant I didn't know if I was ever going to be able to feel for him the way he felt for me. All of these thoughts ran through my mind with a single glance at him in his old camp T-shirt with the sleeves cut off, as he revealed his feelings for me without saying a word.

"So, do you want to go to the beach today?" He asked.

I was pretty sure I was fully awake by now, but I thought I misheard him. "Did you say beach?"

He smiled. "Yep. Rockaway Beach. It's not a far drive from here."

I didn't know what to make of all the new emotions I was feeling, and I was grateful to do anything that did not involve discussing the state of our relationship.

"I didn't know there were beaches near here. That sounds fun. I don't have a bathing suit, though."

Jared shook his head. "You're fine, we can just bring a towel to sit on and hang out."

A short while later we were walking together on a stretch of sand that touched dark, gentle waves at its edge. The beach was quiet. About ten yards to our right, a young, lanky man with a dark beard lay on his stomach on a towel facing out toward the water, a paperback book open in his hands in front of him. Farther away on our left, young parents held the hands of a toddler girl as she took bold but hesitant steps forward in the sand. The sky was clear and the sun was beginning its ascent into the highest point in the sky. Jared slowly unfolded two towels onto the sand, first a faded blue one for him, then a red and blue striped one right next to it for me. I leaned back on my forearms on the towel, my legs stretched in front of me, and Jared lay down on his side facing me on his, his head propped up on his right hand.

I was conscious of Jared looking at me as I gazed out at the water and watched the small waves rolling in and crashing onto the sand, one after another, generating a white foam as the water crept further and further up the beach. It occurred to me that this scene could have been the romantic one that I had wanted so badly the day before. But now, all at once everything felt so serious, and what I had wished for so long was happening too quickly, leaving me lost in an abyss of uncertainty like the deep blue-black water in front of us. While a part of me still felt thrilled to be in Jared's presence and soared with the understanding that he felt the same way for me that I did for him, my enthusiasm still felt cut by a sense of unrest because I couldn't shake the sensation in the pit of my stomach that I had somehow signed up for something that I did not fully understand, as though I had made a major purchase without reading the fine print.

My thoughts were broken up by the sound of Jared's voice now. "See, it's a real beach, right?"

I gave a small laugh. "Indeed it is. It's nice. I definitely did not expect to sit on a beach this weekend."

I snuck a glance at my watch. I was looking forward to having some time to myself on the bus ride home to process the weekend's events, and it was almost time to go.

Right after the beach, Jared drove me to the Port Authority station in Manhattan where I would catch my bus. Soon we were walking through the large metal and glass doors together, then as we approached the gate I saw that a line had already formed at the doorway to the bus garage. This was the exact same spot where I had arrived two days before, filled with so much hope and anticipation to see Jared. Walking here with him now I felt different, changed somehow from the version of me that stood here just forty-eight hours earlier. When we reached the queue, we stopped and faced each other. We shared a long, tight hug, and I felt Jared's black leather jacket crinkle against my body. He smelled clean, like bar soap.

"Talk soon then?" he said with a smile, and I involuntarily smiled back.

"Yes, of course."

I felt wistful all of a sudden as it dawned on me that I didn't know when we would see each other again.

"Bye, Jess," he said casually, before quickly brushing his lips on mine, his relaxed demeanor seeming to presuppose that we would be together again soon.

I touched my lips as I watched him turn and disappear into the crowd of people moving quickly in every direction. The kiss had felt nice, mature somehow.

Soon I sat on the moving bus, watching out the window as the New York City skyline receded into the distance with the beginnings of a pink and gray sunset emanating from behind it. I went over in my mind all that had happened during the weekend. Unsure what to make of my mixed emotions, I tried to savor the memories of the moments I had spent with Jared rather than focus on any apprehensions I had felt. *We kissed. Twice now.* I knew that the weekend had gone exactly as I would have hoped, even if I still didn't know what was yet to come, or what it was that I even wanted.

CHAPTER FIVE

Someone to Look Up at the Stars With

I SIFTED THROUGH THE STACK OF ACCEP-
tance paperwork from New York University that lay in
front of me on the dark green leather blotter, then sat back
in my seat at the oak desk in my parents' family room. *I'm
going to NYU.* I was still wrapping my mind around the
fact that I had selected a school and was now actively making my plans for the fall. My top three contenders had been
George Washington University in DC, NYU, and Boston
University. My brother Mike, a grade behind me in school,
already planned to attend GWU and had made clear that
he wanted to forge his own path without his older sister in
the background—which was fair—so it was between NYU
and BU. After spending several days scouring the Boston
Craigslist page for available apartments near BU, since the
school did not provide housing for transfer students, my

parents and I decided that NYU, which would provide me with a dorm room where I would live amongst the other university sophomores, was the better choice.

In spite of the reservations I had felt about Jared by the time I left New York, I was still optimistic. It was Jared, after all. How could I not be over the moon that he was interested in me? While it would have been nice to have been at the same school as him, particularly because we might also be starting something, choosing NYU also made me feel closer to him since he was from Queens. Since in truth I still didn't know exactly how I saw things panning out for us, though, perhaps this was for the better. I glanced up at the desktop computer in front of me now. Jared and I had talked on the phone sporadically since I returned from New York, but it had been a few days since we had connected. I clicked into the computer and signed on to AIM, and sure enough, there he was: Gr8tefulDd1023. I double clicked on his name to open up a chat window.

> **JeSslcA148:** Hey!
> **Gr8tefulDd1023:** Heya!
> **Gr8tefulDd1023:** How are ya?
> **JeSslcA148:** Good, good
> **JeSslcA148:** So I decided on a school for the fall..I'll be going to NYU :)
> **Gr8tefulDd1023:** Wow! Congrats! =)
> Course I'm disappointed it's not BU, but NYU is great

Gr8tefulDd1023: Also means it'll be easy to find you heh.

JeSslcA148: Yeah :) I imagine you're in New York on occasion

Gr8tefulDd1023: Indeed!

Gr8tefulDd1023: So how's home?

JeSslcA148: It's good! We're about to move up to our lake house for the summer...then I'm headed to camp in a few weeks

Gr8tefulDd1023: Ah, right! How long will you be there for?

JeSslcA148: 8 weeks

It dawned on me now that I was going to be away from Jared for two months, and I still did not know what was going on with us. Was I single? Was I not? All I did know was that I felt mixed emotions about him, so it might be nice to have some clarity before I left. And if we were indeed going to be starting something, it seemed like we should see each other before we couldn't for the rest of the summer. I lightly strummed my hands on the keyboard for moment, debating, before I typed.

JeSslcA148: It would be fun to get together again before I leave.

Gr8tefulDd1023: Definitely! =)

Gr8tefulDd1023: You just traveled here though, I don't want to make you do that again

JeSslcA148: You're always welcome to come here

Gr8tefulDd1023: To Pennsylvania? Hmmmmmm

Gr8tefulDd1023: From what you've described it does sound quite pretty, it might be nice to see it

Gr8tefulDd1023: And you =)

JeSslcA148: That would be awesome! I'll confirm with my parents but I'm sure you could stay with us

JeSslcA148: You let me stay with you, it's only fair

Gr8tefulDd1023: This might be doable

We made a plan for him to visit that weekend. I signed offline and felt excited about the prospect of sharing my hometown with Jared. I looked around the room and realized that if he was going to be here in just a couple of days, I should probably start cleaning now. This was going to be his clearest window into my life, and I wanted it to reflect well. I had never had a boy stay over like this before, and it felt like a big deal. Also, I hoped that seeing him against the backdrop of what I knew would give me the certainty about him that I needed, one way or the other.

"JESS—SOMEONE'S ON THE PHONE FOR YOU!"
I heard my mom's voice ring out from upstairs.

I picked up the receiver in the kitchen. "Hello?"

I heard Jared's voice on the other end, and he sounded dejected.

"Hey Jess. I have some bad news."

My heart sank. I had spent the last three days ferociously cleaning our house, planning out what he and I would do during his visit, and preparing my family accordingly. Was he about to cancel on me?

"I have mono," he finally said resignedly.

I wasn't sure what to think. "Does that mean you can't come?"

Jared hesitated. "Well . . . I feel OK, but I don't want to give it to you."

I felt myself get annoyed now. If he was feeling well, then why couldn't he come? How were we supposed to figure out what was going on between us if he wasn't going to make it? I was leaving for camp soon and this was our last chance to see each other for the rest of the summer. My tone sharpened slightly.

"Oh, well . . . I'm sorry. That's too bad. I was hoping to see you before I left."

Picking up on the edge in my voice, Jared spoke more softly now. "Well, I assumed I shouldn't come because we wouldn't be able to, you know, DO anything."

Aha. Now I understood.

"Oh!" I said. "Well that's fine. It's more about seeing each other before I leave. We can just not DO anything."

Jared's tone brightened. "Really, that's OK with you?"

"It's completely OK," I said confidently. "It would be great if you came."

The air was comfortable between us on the phone now.

"Alright then, it's decided. I'll come."

After I hung up the phone, I sighed, relieved that he was still going to be visiting the next day, mono and all. I had been so excited with all of the preparations for his visit that it would have been an immense disappointment if he didn't come. Now, I felt satisfied that the plan had not changed.

———

I SPENT THE MORNING NERVOUSLY CLEAN-ing the house. Finally, it was almost time for Jared to arrive, and I had nothing left to do but wait. I sat down in the kitchen on a tall stool with a round burgundy seat that was bordered by silver nail heads and put one foot up on the handle of a cabinet below me. I thought about the import of Jared's visit. He was going to see and understand where I came from, everything that made me, me. I looked up at the metal clock on the wall above me, set off by the pink and burgundy-flowered wallpaper behind it. *He should be here any minute.*

All at once my nervous excitement began to morph into a mild panic. *Oh my god. Jared is coming here. He actually just drove four-and-a-half hours to see me and where I grew up.* Suddenly it all felt very weighty, and the apprehensions that had hit me the morning I woke up on his couch in New York slowly creeped back into the pit of my stomach. I took a deep breath. *This is Jared that's coming. You wanted him to visit.* I exhaled again and walked out of the kitchen to look out the dining room window, just in time to see his gray sedan pulling up in front of our house.

———————

I WALKED JARED AROUND INSIDE TO GIVE HIM a tour, then realized that with my family scattered in various rooms, there was no good place for us to be where we could not be overheard. I gestured back toward the front door.

"Do you want to sit out here?"

Moments later we were sitting together on the front steps. I stretched my legs out in front of me and thought about how odd it was that my family never used our front door. It was only opened when company came over for a holiday, or when trick-or-treaters came by on Halloween. Other than that, we always used a small mudroom door off of the driveway. On either side of Jared and me there were two petite white columns that held up a small triangular overhang above the front door. *This is a nice stoop. We should use it more.*

Jared and I sat quietly next to each other at the center of the top step, enjoying the perfectly pleasant early-summer sun and our first moment alone together since he had arrived. His legs were stretched out next to mine, close by but not quite touching. I looked down at my hands and played with the ring on my right pointer finger, a thin silver band filled with tiny marcasite stones that sparkled in the sunlight. The center of the band, instead of following the finger in a full circle, came down into a slight point. The ring had come in a set of three, and was purchased along with my friends Lisa and Mandy toward the end of high school. The rings were meant to be worn together and stacked, but we decided we liked them better individually, so we split the cost and each took a ring. I loved its unique shape and how it reminded me of my friends from home.

Jared saw me fumbling with the ring and reached out his left hand to touch it.

"I like that. It's different." His hand lingered on mine.

"Thanks. I love it." I looked up at him then turned and gazed out at the grass of the community center lawn that fronted our house.

"This is nice," Jared said quietly.

I looked back at him and saw that he was facing me, and I was startled by the look in his blue-gray eyes. They were melting with a deep and sincere affection, just as they had been that morning when I woke up on his couch in Queens. The panic-like pang that I had felt just before I saw him pull up outside our house suddenly sliced back through my gut and began to expand, making a comfortable home deep in my stomach. As I looked back at Jared, I saw the rest of my life reflected back at me in his eyes. Dating through college. Moving to the same city afterward. Engagement. Marriage. A life together. We walked hand in hand down a clear path, our milestones neatly laid out along the paved road. *Is this it? Is this the only person I'm ever going to date?* By now the panic sensation had completely flooded my torso and become an inseparable part of me. *I can't do this.*

I remembered then that Jared had just driven hours to see me and was staying the night. And he was still my close friend. I blinked and snuck another quick look at him before staring back out at the lawn. I had no idea whether or not my change in sentiment was perceptible to him, but I worked to put on my best face to act as though it had not. And these perplexing emotions had come on so fast again that I wasn't sure whether or not they would dissipate just as quickly, and I didn't want to rule anything out.

"Should we head back inside?" I asked.

A little while later, Jared and I were stretched out on the beige leather couch in the family room. My parents and Mike had driven up to our nearby lake house, and Jared and I had hung back to spend some time together before joining them. He lay against the side of the couch with his legs outstretched in front of him and parted, and I sat in their crevice with my back leaning against his chest. The TV was on, but neither of us was really paying attention to it. I felt comfortable if still tentative, grateful that it had already been pre-established that nothing physical was going to happen between us during this visit. As far as Jared knew, nothing had changed, and until I had worked out in my own mind what was going on, I didn't yet feel I was at a place to act as though anything was different.

Soon it was time to meet my family at the lake for dinner. As I drove us down the verdant, circuitous country roads in the dark, I enjoyed being able to share this familiar drive with him. We came upon a particular stretch of the road that runs perfectly straight with large open fields on either side. The jet black sky all around us was thoroughly perforated with tiny sparkly stars. I glanced at Jared in the passenger seat next to me then looked past him at the expanse of tall grass.

"Do you ever see a field like that and have the urge to just stop what you're doing, pull over the car, and lie on your back in the grass and look up at the stars?"

Jared looked at me quickly, startled. "*Right now*?!"

I shook my head. "No. NO! No." I explained as quickly as I could, "I was just saying that I love the idea of doing that, in theory. Someday, at some point. Not right now."

As the car continued down the linear road, the headlight beams glowing in front of us the only source of light besides the stars, I thought about how nice it would be to lay on my back in a field like that, gazing up at the mystery of space with a boy I liked by my side. I still didn't know whether or not that was Jared.

———

WE WALKED INTO THE LAKE COTTAGE TO SEE my parents and brother seated at the round kitchen table, which was covered with a stack of pizza boxes and a few open containers of pasta, bread, and salad. *Mmmm.* The sight was a familiar one for me during the summers. My parents' golden retriever puppy, Sammy, was lying under the table, patiently waiting for any dropped morsels. Jared and I sat down at the table as my mom handed us plates, each with a slice of pizza on it. Sammy jumped up to sniff Jared, excited and curious by the new scent, then started innocuously nibbling his leg.

"Ah, sorry about that," I said to him, then watched with surprise and horror as Jared suddenly stuck his leg entirely underneath Sammy's body and kicked him out of the way with a little bit of force. "Woah," I couldn't help saying. "He's harmless."

"Oh he's fine," Jared replied dismissively.

I looked down at my pizza, slightly stunned. Jared hadn't hurt Sammy in any way, but the attitude with which he had disdainfully kicked him away, like a bug unworthy of his affection, made my stomach drop slightly. I loved animals, and seeing someone I thought I cared about taking an action intended to put an animal in its place alarmed me. This small moment called to mind the various pangs of hesitancy I had felt since spending the weekend with Jared in New York. As I blotted my face with a napkin and watched him take a bite of his pizza, these new doubts joined together with those prior inklings and began swirling together in my mind into a larger force that was beginning to crystallize into a new image of who Jared was to me.

CHAPTER SIX

Not If I Get To Him First

A BUZZ OF CONVIVIAL TALKING AND LAUGH-
ter surrounded me as I filed into the dining hall with counselors ahead of and behind me. I had just arrived at Camp
Laurelwood in Madison, Connecticut that morning. It was
orientation week: one full week of counselor-only instruc-
tion and socializing before the campers arrived. Since that
morning I had met a few of the other counselors. One girl
named Claire and I had clicked immediately, and it was
nice to feel like I had already made a friend. Now, Claire
stood next to me as we entered the log cabin-like dining
room with its ceiling and walls of rich brown wood panel-
ing, the ceiling reaching a peak at the top with supporting
rafters. Parts of the walls and ceiling were covered with various colored pennants and flags from summers of long before. Long wooden picnic-style tables filled the room, and

in the center ran a long, shiny metal buffet with a mod-est-looking salad bar and a few lunch options.

"Where should we sit?" Claire asked me in her British accent.

She was from London but had just finished her second year studying at Princeton University, so her accent was a mix of her British roots and the American intonation she had picked up from her friends at school.

Some counselors had already found seats. There was a contingent of staff from Israel, as is common at Jewish sleepaway camps, and just ahead of me I saw that several of the Israelis were already sitting down together. I paused when I noticed the guy at the end of their table sitting on the side facing me. He was tan, well-built, and extremely attractive. His short brown hair, subtly spiked up in the front with product, matched the brown stubble form-ing the shape of a mustache and beard on his face. What stopped me in my tracks, though, was the huge smile that lit up his entire face, conveying a genuine enthusiasm and thirst for life. His eyes were a deep chocolate brown, with the slight mature air of a young Israeli who had just com-pleted his mandatory army tenure. This was overpowered, though, by the mischievous glint of a young man who was now free to live life on his terms. I wanted to sit by that guy. There were a few available seats on the other side of his table, so I nudged Claire in that direction.

"Let's sit here!"

Claire shuffled in to find a seat on the bench and I slid in next to her at the very end, directly across from the most handsome Israeli I had ever seen. There were several other male counselors around him, and a few Israeli girls sat at the other end of the table. They were all talking and laughing loudly. I smiled at the guy who had caught my eye and held out my hand.

"Hi, I'm Jessica!"

The huge smile that had transfixed me before was now completely focused on me, and I basked in its glow.

"I'm Avi," he said confidently, his deep brown gaze fixed on me as he spoke, the smile unwavering.

His handshake was strong and masculine, and warm and welcoming all at the same time. My hand tingled from his touch. *I need to know this guy.*

———

THE OLD SCREEN DOOR SLAMMED SHUT BE-hind me as I entered the tiny cottage used as a staff lounge. I had told my parents I would check in a few days after I arrived at camp, so I had made my way to the lounge to send them a quick email. I spotted an old computer on a tiny wooden table against the wall to my left with a small chair in front. I sat down in the chair and moved the mouse. I was alone, and the quiet was a welcomed break from the busy past several days of orienting with all of the other counselors.

I had set up a Yahoo account specifically for the summer so I could go on the web and easily check my email. I had only given my new email address to my parents and to Jared, who had asked how he could stay in touch with me during the summer. *Jared.* He had barely crossed my mind since I had arrived at camp. At the moment, I was grateful to have distance from him so I could hopefully, with the passage of time, have a better understanding of how I felt about him. I logged into my account, then went to open a new window to compose an email to my parents. I paused when I saw a new message in my inbox from Jared Glazer, with the subject line "Hey." I sighed. I didn't want to think about him right now. I was enjoying experiencing my new environment and friends, and the last thing I wanted was to feel tied down to something that I wasn't even one hundred percent sure I wanted to be connected to. I knew I would in time have more certainty about Jared one way or the other, and I didn't want to have to make that decision right now. I exhaled again, then clicked the email open.

Hey Jess,

How's it going? You have arrived at camp by now, yes? Look forward to hearing all about it =)

Same as usual here...enjoying bumming around New York for the summer.

Miss you,
Jared

I felt my stomach drop as I read the words "Miss you." Of course he missed me. The last time he checked, we were nearly an item. The pit of my gut began to knot up as I realized the truth. *I don't miss him.* But I also realized that I couldn't just ignore him. *I'll respond later.* I quickly sent off an email to my parents then got up from the chair and headed back out of the staff lounge and into the bright summer day, the screen door closing loudly behind me.

————

"I JUST FEEL LIKE I NEED TO MOVE!" I SAID TO Claire, who was beside me as we walked down a dark paved path that was periodically illuminated with hazy spots of orange glow from the old metal lamp posts lining it on either side.

"I know," she said in her accented English. "I've been literally dying to exercise since we got here."

We had both put on gym shorts and tank tops and decided that regardless of our busy orientation week schedule and the fact that it was now dark out, we needed to exercise and we were going to make it happen now somehow, somewhere. Once I had divulged to her that I had memorized some of the Tae Bo kickboxing moves from my well-loved DVDs back at home, we decided to find a place where we could partake in some much-needed cardio. We eventually came upon the camp's multi-purpose room that we had seen during our camp tour, but we weren't sure if we would have access to it at this hour. We sauntered up to the door and saw a separated metal latch with an open padlock hanging on one side.

Claire looked at me as I shrugged.

"I don't see any harm . . ." she said, so we pushed open the large wooden door.

We stepped tentatively into the expansive, all-wooden room. I blindly felt around on the wall to my left for a light switch. Finally, the room was thoroughly brightened by large neon lights shining from above, and it no longer felt like we were trespassing. The space was completely empty except for a few scattered foldable metal chairs. One wall was covered with more folded and stacked chairs, and to our right was a large wooden stage.

"Well, this is perfect," I said nodding slowly. "We can sweat and look ridiculous, and no one will see us."

About twenty minutes into some bouncing, jumping, and kick-punch combos, we suddenly paused at the sound of boisterous laughing and talking immediately outside. Claire and I both looked toward the heavy wood door that we had left partially open and watched as it was pushed in further and the full contingent of seven male and female Israeli counselors poured inside, their loud and fun-loving energy palpable in the summer evening air. I felt myself instinctively smile when I saw the mischievous glimmer of Avi's eyes and his full grin, and then looked away, trying not to show my excitement that he had just walked in. The day I met him I had learned that he was twenty-three, which felt like a vast age difference from me at nineteen, but which had only served to enhance his intrigue.

An older counselor, also named Avi, and whom Claire and I had dubbed "Big Avi," was eyeing us curiously. Big Avi received his nickname because he was heads taller than everyone else, and also a few years older than even the original Avi. His head was shaved and he had a massive build with broad shoulders. He would come across as intimidating, but his rough-looking exterior was cut by the pleasant sweetness of his demeanor. Now, he raised his eyebrows at us and smiled slowly.

"Whaaaat are you ladies doing in here?"

I saw Claire blush slightly and I reflexively smoothed back the sweaty flyaways in my hair.

"Just working out," I said, as Claire lightly shifted her weight from her right foot to her left, stretching out her leg muscles.

"Really?" Big Avi exaggeratedly suppressed laughter. "Well, do you guys mind if we put some music on in here?"

I smiled. Avi was already up on the stage off to the side, fiddling with the sound system.

"Not at all!" I said, figuring we were essentially done working out anyway.

Seconds later, before we could get another word out, the fast-paced *thump thump thump* of Israeli techno music was blaring from the speakers in the upper corners of the room. First the Israeli guys, then also the girls, were now jumping to the beat, free from inhibition. They had truly brought the party, and their energy was infectious. Claire and I started bouncing in place to the music now, too.

Thump thump thump. The deep bass was sprinkled with fast-paced drum beats and occasional Hebrew lyrics. Claire and I danced in a way that I thought was standard, moving somewhat delicately to the music, mostly in place. We both had a natural instinct to hold back slightly, to not have everything out on the table. The Israelis, though, they were dancing like I had never seen anyone dance before, moving quickly, aimlessly, and with complete and utter abandon. Several of the guys were spinning around in circles as fast as they could, arms outstretched. To them, there was no camp outside those doors, no larger world beyond the entrance, no anxiety about what was to come in their lives, post-army service. There was only right here, in this moment, with this beat. Their now sweat-streaked faces careened by effortlessly, their bodies bouncing every which way in a beautiful kind of chaos.

Before long, even Claire and I had cast aside our inhibitions and were dancing as freestyle and silly as they were. As I felt myself jumping higher and higher to the music, having the time of my life, I was conscious of how special and spontaneous the moment was; one that would likely never be replicated. *Thump thump thump thump thump.* I didn't even care that Avi was there and could see me as I spun in place now, my dried kickboxing sweat misted with a new glow. I laughed and realized that this was the best I had felt in a long time. I was truly leaving behind everything in my life outside these wood-paneled multi-purpose room walls. There was no more worrying or wondering how I felt about Jared or what was going to happen next in my life at school. There was nothing else besides this music, these faces, this space, and this night, and I had never felt so free.

———

IT WAS ANOTHER NIGHTFALL OF COUNSELOR orientation week, and Claire and I found ourselves looking for something to do. We had had so much fun with the group of Israeli counselors the night before, and I was hoping to see them again tonight. Specifically, I was hoping to get a chance to talk to Avi. We decided to plant ourselves on a swing set that was ideally situated just off the main walking path, where others would be likely to spot us.

"Wait, but, you call it a boot?!" I was saying to Claire, who had just explained to me that where she was from, the storage area at the back of a vehicle was called a "boot" rather than a "trunk."

We were each sitting on a swing, moving back and forth slowly as we chatted. It was a perfect, clear summer night. A low background chorus of crickets chirped in the distance, and the dark night air was occasionally punctuated by the brilliant yellow-green glow of a lightning bug announcing its presence. After a little while, I saw a few of the Israeli counselors walking down the path in our direction, Avi's standout build noticeable among them. I felt the warm glow of excitement rise in my chest when they stopped to hang out by the swings where we were.

I looked over at Avi standing by himself several yards from me, near one of the metal poles staking the swing set into the ground.

"So how did you end up at this camp?" I asked him.

He smiled back at me with a furrowed brow, and I could tell that my words had gotten lost amidst the other cheerful conversation happening around us. He walked toward me so that he was standing just in front of the swing I was sitting on.

I held onto the metal chains on either side of me as I looked up at him.

"So how did you end up here?" I asked again.

He smiled. "Ah, yes," he said in his heavily accented English. "I was in the army for a long time; I stayed on as an officer. That's why I'm older than some of the others here." He smiled again as I nodded and met his grin. "I knew I wanted to work with kids, and this was a great way to start traveling once I was done with the army."

The full moon overhead cast a faint blue-white light over his intense facial features as he spoke.

I told him about my own trajectory that had led me to the camp then said, "I really want to learn Hebrew. I'm hoping I can pick some up from you guys this summer."

His eyes gleamed and his smile broadened. "Oh yeah? I can teach you."

My face lit up, my feet drawing small left and right horizontal lines into the gravel below.

"What do you want to learn how to say?" he asked.

I looked up at the full moon above and then back down at Avi, savoring the idyllic moment. "How do you say 'the moon looks beautiful tonight'?"

His signature smile spread across his face again before he turned and glanced up at the moon then back at me. "Hi-yareach . . . ye-feh . . . me-od."

I repeated it back. "Hi-yareach . . . ye-feh . . . me-od."

We smiled at each other in silence for a moment before I was startled by the sound of uproarious laughter from the others around us. I had lost sight of the fact that anyone else was even with us; for those precious moments of my conversation with Avi, it had been just him, me, and the moon. And the moon looked beautiful tonight.

———

THE AFTERNOON SUN RADIATED A BRIGHT light through the window of the small camp exercise room. Orientation week was nearly complete, and Claire and I were enjoying some much-needed downtime. Feeling slightly pent-up, we again sought out an opportunity to exercise. When we arrived at the small shed and saw that it was filled with only a few weight machines, a bored Claire started showing me some basic ballet steps as I imitated her. My legs were now bent into a plie position, my arms curved in a downward circular shape.

"This is fun!" I said. "Maybe I'll take adult ballet."

Suddenly the old door to the shed squeaked open. Claire and I turned our heads in that direction in unison. In waltzed Avi in a T-shirt and athletic shorts.

"What are you guys doing? Up to no good?" he asked, amused.

I internally marveled at how all Avi needed to do was walk into a room with that luminous smile, his eyes sparkling as though he was in on some sort of perennial secret and the air was instantly ignited with a new, exciting energy. Our afternoon had shifted from ordinary to interesting. *We keep running into him.*

Claire and I quit doing ballet for the moment, and the three of us lounged on exercise equipment and chatted. Avi began telling us more about his life before camp. We learned that as soon as he got out of the army, he had done some traveling with his serious girlfriend at the time. *At the time.* He pulled a picture out of his wallet, and I leaned over to see the photo. Avi and a girl, both wearing hiking gear, sat side by side on a large rock at the top of a high mountaintop with rolling green hills spread out below them.

"This is her," he said.

As I looked at the photo, I thought about how magnificent it would feel to be that girl, sitting on a rock with Avi somewhere majestically beautiful with the entire world below.

"But it was the right thing for it to end," I heard Avi say, and I was jolted out of my musing as he described how they had broken up just before he came to the states for camp.

I watched his face as he talked. He seemed like such a grown and experienced man, and I wanted to learn from him, to have my own taste of what he knew about the world.

———

BEFORE LONG, THE STAFF ORIENTATION PERI-od was over, and camp had officially begun. The campers had been dropped off, hugged and kissed by their parents. Summer at camp consisted of two universes—one during the day, when I was in charge of a group of campers, and the other at night, when the campers slept and us counselors had an entire world of our own. Each night, a few counselors were assigned to be on duty and patrol the bunk areas occasionally to make sure nothing was awry, but those that weren't on duty were free for the evening. Since we were able to choose our night patrol shifts, we could sign up with counselors that we wanted to work with. I had taken to the Israeli counselors, and I found myself spending most of my time with them, along with Claire and a couple other female counselors from Italy. There was another entire cohort of counselors that hung out together, all from the states, who knew each other from attending the camp as kids.

Tonight, I sat on the front porch of the "on duty" station along with two female Israeli counselors I had become good friends with, Michal and Tamar. The "on duty" station was a small cabin located midway through the large semicircle of girls' bunks that faced an open grassy area. Across the field was a building housing bathrooms, sinks, and showers, and the entire section was separated from the boys' area of camp by a hill in the middle with a flagpole at the top.

The three of us sat in white plastic chairs with our feet up on the wood railing in front of us as we looked out into the night. The "on duty" cabin provided the ideal vantage point for spotting a light clicking on in a bunk or a stray camper, but the girls' section of camp was still now, with only the occasional lightning bug twinkling in the open field before us. Tamar was telling us about her boyfriend back home in Israel.

"We've been together a long time now. He's the one." She smiled, her dark eyes sparkling. Now she looked at me. "What about you, Jessica? Do you have a boyfriend?"

I sighed at the question and brought my left foot onto the seat of my chair and wrapped my arms around my knee. "Well, there is a guy I sort of just started something with before I came here," I told them. "But I'm not really sure where I want it to go."

Michal and Tamar both looked at me, listening carefully.

"It felt like it started to get really serious really quickly, so I decided to just take the summer to think about it by not really thinking about it. You know?"

Both girls nodded back at me.

Tamar gave me a serious look. "I think when you know, you know," she said solemnly. "You just have to decide if you feel it . . . you know, down there, when you're with him." She gestured toward her crotch. "That's how you know."

I looked at her quizzically, and Michal burst out laughing. But Tamar's face was resolute, her deep brown eyes fixed on me as she nodded, no trace of humor anywhere about her. I smiled and looked back out at the darkness. The moonlight had cast a preternatural glow on the branches of the several tall trees on the girls' camp.

"Yeah, I don't know. I'm just glad I don't have to make a decision right now."

Tamar shook her head firmly. "No. You don't."

———

IT WAS NIGHTTIME AGAIN—OR COUNSELOR happy hour. I stood on the paved path that wound its way through camp along with Claire, Avi, and several other counselors clustered into small groups. Avi and a few other guys decided to break away to go play video games in the staff lounge. As soon as they were gone, another counselor named Emily ran up to me. She had a broad build and long, reddish-brown, tight curly hair. She technically fell into the "Americans that attended Camp Laurelwood as kids" cohort of counselors who largely kept to themselves, but she made her way around to the other cliques, and I had become friendly with her. She loved being in on all of the counselor gossip, and since we were all spending the summer together in middle-of-nowhere Connecticut without much else to do besides what we had in front of us, it was hard to keep much of anything a secret. I hadn't told anyone besides Claire that I was interested in Avi, but somehow Emily knew.

And now she stood squarely in front of me, nearly breathless as she looked at me and lowered her voice. "You know, you're not the only one who likes Avi," she said gravely.

I tried to look surprised as I raised my eyebrows at her. "Oh yeah?"

She shook her head. "Orly likes him too. And she knows you like him, so she decided she's going to try to get to him first."

I furrowed my brow, trying to unpack all that Emily had just said. *Orly?* Orly was another counselor from the states, but she had not attended camp before, so she wasn't part of that circle. She didn't hang out with me and the foreigners either; she was more of a floater. A couple of years younger than me, she was pretty with long, straight, light brown hair parted in the middle, big blue-green eyes, and a large mouth. She was offbeat, a bit hippy-ish, and somewhat aloof, and I hadn't interacted with her much, mostly because we simply hadn't had that much to say to each other. I thought she was nice enough, but who knew she had it out for me?

I simply stared at Emily, who had more to say.

"Yeah, she said she knows you like him because she saw you guys talking and you were sticking your chest out."

OK, wait. What? I don't even know what that means. I shook my head, confused. "OK . . . well . . . thanks for telling me?"

Emily nodded and ran off, clearly pleased with what she had done. I remained standing in the same place, looking at where Emily had just been and thinking about what she had said—that Orly was going to try and get to Avi first.

For a moment I simply felt annoyed. *Why is Orly so interested in my business? We've barely even spoken.* Then, I felt my heart start beating faster as adrenaline began circulating through my body and my annoyance gave way to anger. Things had only just started with Avi. They most certainly weren't going to end this way. Not now, not yet, and not because of Orly. I looked toward the staff lounge. Just outside to the right, Orly was standing with a couple other female counselors. I looked back at the door, remembering that Avi was inside. I turned, stood up straight, and quickly marched up to the staff lounge, not acknowledging Orly's group as I passed. *Not if I get to him first.* I pulled open the screen door and went inside.

In the back of the cottage, there was a small room with an old TV set. I found Avi there with a couple other male counselors, sitting on hard plastic chairs in front of the screen. Avi had a video game controller in his hand, and they were all staring intently at the TV. They looked up at me with surprise now as I burst into the room.

"Hey!" I said. "Video games?"

"Awww yeahhh," Avi said, his eyes back on the TV again as he tipped the controller to the left and then followed with his whole body as he moved the avatar across the screen.

They were all looking back at the game now, my presence irrelevant. I thought about Orly just outside the staff lounge, waiting for Avi to finish playing video games so she could find him and do whatever "getting to him first" meant. Time was of the essence. I walked up to Avi and sat down on one of his open legs, facing inward, right next to where he was holding the controller.

"Oh, hey!" he said, looking at me now.

"Can I hang out here until you're done?" I asked innocently.

"Suuuure," Avi said, now visibly distracted from the game.

I had trouble hiding my smile; his stubble was so close to my face, and I could smell his fresh, clean scent. I had no idea what was supposed to happen next, or what exactly I even wanted to happen. But warm adrenaline was still buzzing in my veins, and I knew two things—first, that I had to beat Orly at whatever game she had just created for us, and second, that I had to get to Avi before I lost my chance. Fortunately, these two goals were completely intertwined.

Avi continued playing the video game for a few more minutes, but the message I had sent by jumping onto his lap had been received by the room. Soon the others left the staff lounge entirely and only the two of us remained. We moved into the main room and sat next to each other on an old, 1970s-looking couch covered in tiny vertical stripes of various oranges, yellows, and browns. The couch had several tears in its surface and was clearly loved in a past life before being donated to this cottage in lieu of being discarded. On one cushion, a large gash had exposed a sizable chunk of the dull yellow foam from inside.

Avi slid over closer to me so that the striped fabric was no longer visible between us, and I felt my heart beating rhythmically. We talked idly for a moment or two, the words meaningless. He turned to face me and reached for my left hand, and I looked up at him, and then we were kissing. Just like that. I was sitting to Avi's left, leaning my back against the couch, with only my face turned toward his. My right cheek was pressed against the couch cushion behind me, and I wondered for a moment whether the lines in the old fabric were imprinting onto my face. Avi was in the exact but reverse position to my right. Our posture felt awkward, but I didn't shift out of fear that it would ruin the moment.

The kiss was equally as wonderful as it was artless. I enjoyed the feeling of Avi's full lips on my own, and I loved the taste of his mouth, even though there were traces of cigarette smoke, which I had not experienced before but also surprisingly did not mind. I was kissing a gorgeous Israeli man who was more mature than any of my peers back home, and if that came with an ashtray-like aftertaste, then that was just part of the package. I became aware that my whole chin was covered in saliva somehow, but I simply wiped my face with my right hand, and we kept on kissing.

All of a sudden, we jumped at the sound of the screen door to the staff lounge creaking open loudly. Avi and I quickly separated from each other on the couch before looking behind us to see that one of the American male counselors had sat down at the computer to check his email. I quickly wiped my face again, this time on the end of my sleeve, then smoothed down my mussed hair. I knew my face must have been bright red, but I didn't care. I was walking on air, intoxicated from the moment with Avi.

We quickly said good night to each other before leaving the cabin, and headed in opposite directions toward our respective bunks. As I stuck my hands in the back pockets of my denim shorts and walked briskly, the balmy summer evening air perfectly reflected the warmth I felt inside. I couldn't wait for what the rest of the summer would bring.

———

THE SUN SHONE BRIGHTLY OVER THE LARGE rectangular pool, which reflected back gold in its small ripples of water. The pool, the deck, and the grass surrounding it were filled with noisy campers receiving a swimming lesson from the camp instructor. It had been a couple days since Avi and I had kissed in the staff lounge, and I had been walking around blissfully content during that time. Now, I stood in the shade behind a small pool shed with Michal, Ronit, and Tamar, who had by now become three of my favorite people at camp. Ronit, like Michal and Tamar, was also part of the Israeli contingent, and we were all enjoying some downtime together while the swim instructor was in charge of our campers.

"Jessica." Tamar stretched out her arms and put one hand on each of my shoulders. She stared at me with her serious, chocolate brown eyes. "I talked to Avi," she said in her accented English. "He likes you."

I felt myself blush as I smiled and gazed down for a moment before looking back up at her.

"OK. Well, I like him too."

Nodding, she continued, "But, he wants to have sex this summer. That's what he told me. He is recently out of a serious relationship, and that's all he's looking for right now."

I felt the smile quickly disappear from my face, the magic dissipating just as quickly as it had come. "Oh!" I said, and she added quickly, "I told him I didn't think that's what you were looking for, and you probably wanted something more than that."

I nodded slowly, my lips pursed. "Well, you're right."

And she was. I was immediately put off by the thought that Avi was exclusively looking for something physical. I felt my heart sink as I began to understand that even though I liked him and saw the potential for something great, if the timing wasn't right, then it wasn't going to be. As much as I wanted to, I couldn't be that girl with him on the boulder at the top of the mountain because he wasn't ready for that yet.

Tamar was still holding my shoulders, looking at me with her brow furrowed and genuine concern in her eyes. "If that's all he's looking for, then you don't want to be with him anyway. I don't want you to get hurt. Are you OK?"

I sighed. "Yeah. Just disappointed." I sat down on the narrow wooden ledge that ran alongside the pool shed.

Michal sat down next to me and draped an arm over my shoulders. "Don't worry. He's not that great," she said with a smile.

"Yeah . . ." I said, slowly dragging a tiny stick along in the dirt on the ground in front of me.

I felt disenchanted; it all seemed unfair. If Avi and I liked each other, why couldn't that be enough, even if the timing wasn't perfect? I wanted so badly to kiss him again, to keep kissing him, to continue what we had started that night in the staff lounge. I wanted to learn more Hebrew from him, I wanted to learn more about the world from him. I wanted to look up at the moon with him again. Tamar's words replayed in my mind. "He wants to have sex this summer . . . that's all he's looking for right now." I again felt unease in the pit of my stomach.

Tamar sat down on my other side. "Orly likes Avi too, and he knows that," she continued in her solemn voice. "And he knows that she will probably sleep with him."

I sighed deeply. If what Tamar had told me moments ago had been a punch to my gut, now hearing this, I just felt entirely hollow. *Orly. Well, at least I got to him first.* I mustered a small smile. "Fine with me if she has my sloppy seconds." I tried to make my voice sound lighthearted, but I knew I couldn't hide my disappointment.

"I'VE ALWAYS WONDERED ABOUT A NOSE piercing, like if I could pull it off," I said as I ran my hand over the glass display case on the counter in front of me, peering at the tiny crystal studs.

It was Fourth of July weekend, and I was in New York City with some of the Israeli counselors. I had coordinated my time off from camp with Michal and Ronit, with a few of the male counselors joining us, and we all traveled to New York together by train. Avi was not with us, which was probably for the better at this point, but "Big Avi" was.

Presently, Big Avi had decided he wanted both of his ears pierced, so the group of us had wandered into a tiny tattoo and piercing shop near SoHo. Ronit studied my face now.

"Yes! It would look so cute on you!" she said in broken English.

"Ahh! You have to do it!" Michal chimed in. "It will be a great memory from our trip. Let's pick one out right now."

Before I knew it, I was sitting in a ripped black faux leather chair in a small room with walls covered in stickers with band names on them. I looked at myself in the large rectangular mirror on the wall just in front of me and took a deep breath.

"Well I guess I have no choice now, right?"

Big Avi, who was in the room with us now, nodded, a new shiny metal stud in each ear. "Yep. Peer pressure, man."

I looked around at my new friends. Michal. Ronit. Big Avi. And another counselor named Elad, who had woken up at 6 a.m. that morning, and by his own words, "walked across the entirety of Manhattan, bottom to top." Ronit was shaking her fists in the air excitedly. I reached up and touched the tiny silver hoop at the top of my left ear. I cherished the memories from my USY trip to Israel that the earring regularly regenerated for me. I realized that if I was ever going to get a nose piercing, this was the perfect occasion. It would allow me to commemorate this moment, in this place, with these wonderful people.

Walking back out into the daylight with a new tiny clear crystal on the right side of my nose, I felt completely and utterly happy. Any time spent away from camp was a breath of fresh air; camp was such a bubble that it was always restorative to have a reminder of the world outside its confines. And today, I was having a great time. The group of us wandered the streets together a while longer with no agenda to speak for; the city was ours to explore.

Eventually, Michal, Ronit and I separated from the others to drop off our things at the place we were staying that night. After we entered a tall building somewhere in Midtown and rode up in an elevator together, Michal looked at us.

"Remember, it's actually an office. But my cousin said we are welcome to sleep here."

Ronit and I both shrugged. We were all having so much fun in the city, and I was grateful to have a place to sleep at all. After we walked down a short hallway, Michal stuck a key into a gold doorknob. As she pushed open the door, we all peered inside. The narrow, rectangular room stretched out in front of us with textured maroon carpet on the floor below. Some small cubicles and filing cabinets were scattered along the walls, and there were stacks of paper all around. We stepped inside.

"This is great!" I said as I dropped my backpack on the floor. "And we have it all to ourselves. Thanks, Michal."

The three of us sat down in black swivel desk chairs that we had moved to the center of the room.

"So what are we doing tonight?" Ronit wondered aloud.

It was the Fourth of July, but we had no plans.

I rotated my chair slowly from left to right. "I'm fine with whatever. We can walk around. Order food." I caught a glimpse of a desktop computer in the cubicle to my left, and then I looked at Michal. "Hey, is it OK if I use this for a minute?"

She was studying her nails and barely looked up to see what I was referring to. "Yeah, sure. Just don't break it, I guess?"

I used my feet to slowly roll my desk chair around the corner and into the cubicle. When I turned on the computer, I saw that AOL Instant Messenger was installed on the desktop. I hadn't been on AIM all summer. Jared had barely been on my mind at all since I had been at camp, but being in New York, it was admittedly hard not to think of him. Walking the streets with my Israeli friends that afternoon had reminded me of when I strolled the streets with him just months before, and I felt a pang of guilt now being in the city without him knowing. I took a deep breath and signed into my AIM account.

My eyes immediately darted to the top righthand corner of the screen to scan my Buddy List. There it was, right at the top—Gr8tefulDd1023. *Cha-ching.* I thought with wonder about how we had been apart all summer, but now I was sitting so close to where he physically was. I knew if he spotted me online, he would be surprised and want an explanation, and I would have to tell him where I was. Also, much of the city was still largely foreign to me, and also to my Israeli friends, but it was Jared's home. I exhaled again, so loudly that Ronit glanced up at me briefly from the other end of the room before slouching back into her desk chair and spinning around toward the window to gaze outside. I double clicked on Jared's name to open up a new message window.

    JeSslcA148: Hey!

He replied almost immediately.

    Gr8tefulDd1023: Heya!! =) Long time no
    talk! Glad to see you on here
    JeSslcA148: Yeah, I know it's been a while
    JeSslcA148: So I'm actually in NYC right
    now....
    Gr8tefulDd1023: !!!! What
    JeSslcA148: Yeah. At the last minute I came
    in for a couple days with some friends from
    camp
    Gr8tefulDd1023: Does this mean I get to
    see you??

I thought about how Michal, Ronit, and I had no plans for the evening. I didn't want to give Jared the wrong idea by seeing him when I still wasn't sure how I felt about him.

I was supposed to be using the summer away to figure that out, but maybe seeing him now would be informative, since some time had passed after all. And at the very least, weren't we friends?

> **JeSslcA148:** Well, I'm headed back to camp tomorrow morning. I know it's the 4th and you might be busy, but we're free tonight?

I felt my breathing quicken. I wasn't sure how I wanted him to respond; I didn't know if I wanted him to be free or not.

> **Gr8tefulDd1023:** Hmm. I was supposed to meet up with a friend, but let me fix that. I'm not going to miss you if you're in my city. Hang on.

I looked over at Michal and Ronit. "Hey guys, I might have a friend that wants to meet up with us. It's my friend Jared," I explained. "Michal, you might remember, I told you about him. We were kinda dating before camp started."

Her face lit up. "Yes! We get to meet him??"

I looked back down at the computer. "Possibly. Give me a second."

Ronit had slid her desk chair away from the window, rolled back across the room, and was now right next to me. "Can he take us to see fireworks somewhere??" she asked eagerly, her light blue eyes glistening with childlike hope.

I glanced down at the computer screen again and saw that Jared had returned.

> **Gr8tefulDd1023:** Okay, I'm free now. I'm all yours. Where are you?

After I described where we were staying, I told him about Ronit's request.

> **JeSslcA148:** My friends are Israeli and they want to experience a true American Fourth of July, like fireworks and stuff...do you know of any that are close by?
> **Gr8tefulDd1023:** I'm sure I can come up with something...
> **Gr8tefulDd1023:** I can get to you at 8:00 and pick you guys up, and bring you back after. Does that work?

I checked with the other girls, who were overjoyed to have someone who knew the city to take us to see fireworks. Michal was fluffing up her tight brown curly hair now and straightening out her shirt.

> **JeSslcA148:** Yes, that's perfect. We'll see you then!

A little while later we climbed into Jared's sedan. I said a quick hello when I sat down in the passenger seat, and felt grateful that Michal and Ronit were chatting him up excitedly from the back of the car, diffusing any ambiguity in the air between the two of us up front.

Soon, we pulled into a small parking lot somewhere in Queens where Jared knew that a fireworks show was happening. We quickly stepped outside just in time to see the first few bursts of white flash in the sky before slowly dissipating into the black night. Jared walked around the car to stand next to me, and Michal and Ronit stood just behind us. *Boom, pop. Boom, pop.* Sprinkles of colored light lit up the dark sky, now red, then blue. Out of the corner of my eye, I saw Jared step closer to me, then just as quickly, I felt his arm slide around my upper back. I turned and looked at his face, so close to mine now.

"I like the new look," he whispered and then gestured toward my nose.

"Thanks," I said with a quick smile before gazing back up at the sky.

I wasn't sure what to think. I glanced over my shoulder at Michal and Ronit, who were now watching us and talking quietly. I felt conspicuous with Jared's arm around me. *Why is he acting like we're a couple? I don't know what we are, but it's not that.* I noticed that Jared had turned his head and was watching me again. I took a deep breath and continued watching the sky. *Boom, BOOM, boom, sizzle.* Tiny white sparkles trickled every which way now before melting into the darkness. I suddenly felt Jared's hand by my chin.

"Hey," he said softly.

When I turned toward him, in an instant he placed his lips softly on mine for a brief kiss. *Woah. Wait, woah woah woah.* I peeked back over my shoulder at the girls, who looked ecstatic. Michal was doing a small dance in place and clapping her hands, and when she caught my eye she pointed toward Jared and then gave me an overdramatic thumbs up sign.

I felt myself blush, but not because I was touched by the kiss. I just felt embarrassed as I stared straight ahead. I hated that Jared was acting like we were something that I wasn't sure about. He was demonstrating that he liked me, but it just made me uncomfortable. After a rapid fire of colorful bursts in the sky, one right after another in time— *pop pop pop BOOM BOOM pop hiss hiss*—the sky settled back to dark and the air was quiet around us. A few people clapped and cheered. I swiftly pulled away from Jared, in fear of another kiss or a conversation that I wasn't ready for.

"OK, so we should probably be getting back!" I said quickly as I opened my car door and turned toward Michal and Ronit.

Ronit was holding up a small silver camera. "Wait, we need a picture!" she said excitedly.

"Here, I'll take it," Jared volunteered. He took the camera and walked a few yards ahead to the curb before turning around and crouching down low to the ground. He looked through the camera's tiny lens.

Click. The moment was captured. Because of Jared's position, the camera was angled up at the three of us, making us look taller. I stood in the middle, clad in khaki shorts and a black tank top, my hair pulled back, and sporting the new tiny sparkle in the side of my nose. Michal, with her dark curls, and Ronit, with her long, straight blonde hair, were on either side of me. We each had wide, happy smiles, our eyes shining with the playful excitement of our weekend escapade away from camp. Jared was out of the picture, actually and figuratively. The photograph, like the whole evening, was entirely about Michal, Ronit, and me. Jared was merely a facilitator, off-camera, out of the shot.

Jared's car crawled slowly through the Manhattan traffic on our way back to Michal's cousin's office. After we pulled up to the curb out front, I swiftly opened my door.

"Thanks so much for taking all of us, that was fun!" I said to Jared. "Talk to you soon." I clicked the door closed, grateful that Michal and Ronit were with me so I could avoid a protracted goodbye.

As the three of us stood on the sidewalk and watched him drive away, Ronit walked up next to me and slung her arm around my shoulder. She turned and faced me with a deep sincerity in her ice blue eyes. "He really . . . loves you," she said in her slightly broken English.

My heart felt heavy. *Love?* I was still trying to figure out whether or not I liked Jared romantically at all. The thought of him loving me, if it were even true, made me feel slightly anxious, but also suddenly sorry for how I had treated him. He had gone out of his way to see me tonight on a dime, and even canceled other plans, when I had been slow to reply to his emails all summer. Ronit's words were said so firmly and surely, and with a trademark Israeli gravitas. I knew they were true.

———————

I LIFTED MY HEAD, FLUFFED MY PILLOW, AND turned to lay on my other side, attempting to get comfortable in my twin-sized camp bed. A sliver of moonlight peeked in from the side of the thin curtain on the window just above the head of my bed. The campers in my bunk had long since drifted off to sleep, and I lay awake trying to shake the image of Avi and Orly together from my mind.

After returning from New York, I had quickly learned through the counselor rumor mill that they were an item. I hadn't seen them together yet, but we were all busy with our campers' activities during the days. Earlier this evening though, I had been hanging out with a large group of counselors and the two of them were conspicuously missing. Apparently they were already regularly sleeping together, and a small shed far out on the archery field was the choice of venue for their rendezvous. I wished I didn't have that information, but camp was just too small of a place. Everyone knew.

I burrowed my head deeper into my pillow now and finally started to doze off. All of a sudden I was awakened by the sound of gravel crunching under the weight of footsteps on the walkway right outside my window. It sounded like the alternating footsteps of two people. *Crunnnnch, crunnnnch, crunnnnch* went their feet, until they stopped at what sounded like the bunk next door. I felt my stomach sink as I remembered that Orly worked in that bunk. *Orly and Avi.* No one else would be walking around at this time of night unless they were sneaking around. I heard some low talking now. One of the voices clearly sounded like Orly, who was not a soft-spoken person. Next came the slow *creeeeeeeak* of a bunk door being carefully opened and then shut. Then I heard one set of footsteps retreat back in the direction from which they had come. I felt each increasingly distant *crunnnnch, crunnnch, crunnnch* of Avi's steps on the hard gravel as if it was physically pressing into my heart.

I was aghast that I had just heard the two of them, right outside my window, returning from a late-night archery shed tryst. Just because I knew where they probably were and what they were likely doing didn't mean that I was ready to hear them, right there, right after the fact, literally right outside my window, right under my nose, essentially right in front of my face. I had liked Avi in what felt like a real, adult way, and it wasn't supposed to end like this. Was I going to have to experience this, right outside my window, for the rest of the summer? I hadn't even been able to get over him yet; since I saw him every day, my feelings hadn't yet had a chance to dissipate. They had never even gotten to fully materialize; our chance had been so quickly aborted.

I lay with my left cheek on the pillow and my eyes open wide now. I blinked and briefly flashed back to the Fourth of July, when Jared drove away from Michal, Ronit and me.

He really loves you. I sighed and turned onto my stomach, my face pressed into the pillow. How strange it was to be hurting someone and to also be hurt by someone else at the same time, during the same summer.

———

I HELD ON TIGHTLY TO THE CHAINS ON EIther side of my swing, my feet anchored in the soil in front of me as I absentmindedly moved slowly back and forth.

"I really liked him," I told Claire, who was sitting on the swing beside me.

"I know," she said simply.

We sat in silence for a few minutes as I continued moving gingerly forward and backward. It had been raining earlier in the day, so the air was brisker than normal now. The black asphalt of the walkway that we faced was shiny under the warm glow of the lamp posts. I thought with some sadness about how, just weeks before, I had sat on this very swing and looked up at the full moon with Avi as he taught me some Hebrew. How things had changed since then.

"At least you don't have Big Avi after you like I do," Claire said suddenly, and I laughed, appreciating the comic relief.

This was true—Big Avi had, by this point in the summer, become deeply enamored by Claire, but unfortunately for him, he was simply not her type.

"Aww, he really likes you!" I said.

She nodded slowly. "I know. And I'm trying to figure out what to do about it. He's just such a big teddy bear, so I don't want to hurt his feelings." She pulled back in her swing before letting her feet go and springing forward into the air slightly. "I like him, just not like THAT."

I saw a figure ahead, walking down the asphalt path toward where we were sitting. As the person approached closer, I recognized Nora, a woman who worked in the camp office. She was older than us by at least twenty years or so, and her light brown hair was cropped short near her ears. She noticed that we were sitting quietly away from the other counselors, and stopped in front of us now.

"What's wrong, ladies?"

I looked down at my feet still pointed in the soil then used my legs to move my swing backward and sighed. "Oh, nothing."

Claire looked up at her and said quickly, "Boy trouble."

Nora carefully looked us over. "Well, I don't know what happened, but what I can tell you is that this, too, shall pass." She zipped up her windbreaker and continued on her way down the path.

I looked out blankly into the distance in the direction of the archery field. *This too shall pass.*

———

IT WAS DIFFICULT SEEING AVI AND ORLY TO-gether for the remainder of the summer, but fortunately they ended up spending most of their time with Karen and the other American counselors while I kept to my original group with Claire and the rest of the Israeli staff. I carefully avoided Avi on an individual basis to the best of my ability, but strangely as the summer went on, I eventually got to know Orly somewhat and found I did not dislike her. We discovered a shared love for the band Dispatch, and during one overlapping day off from camp, she invited several other counselors and me to her parents' house in Connecticut. I suppose that over the course of a long summer, some things can change. I never felt comfortable around Avi again, though. It still felt like I had been wronged by him somehow.

Eventually, the summer came to an end. The campers were picked up by their parents and driven back to their respective homes, and there were a couple days left when the counselors were required to stay at camp to clean up and disassemble things. These were the last hours that all of us would spend together before we departed on our separate life paths. It was more difficult to avoid Avi during this time without the diffusion of a full camp around us. The quiet of the scenery reminded me of orientation week when I had first met him, when we had flirted and I was excited about what the summer might bring. Now, I was just looking forward to not having to see him ever again.

And now, on the last day, I stood in my empty bunk and swept one last small pile of dirt into a dustpan and then dumped it into a large white trash bag. I tied the bag into a tight knot and carried it out to the front porch, leaving it along with the broom and dustpan resting against the front of the cabin. I quickly dashed down the wooden steps from the porch but somehow landed incorrectly on one of my feet, and before I knew it, I was on my hands and knees on the concrete platform below.

"Owww!" I yelled, sitting up on the concrete with my left leg bent so I could inspect my freshly scraped knee. I suddenly heard an Israeli-accented male voice just over me.

"Wow, Jess, are you OK?"

I looked up to see Avi standing above me, looking equal parts amused and concerned.

Avi. Of course. The last person I would want to see me wipe out. I composed my face and stood up, brushing off my hands and then legs.

"I'm fine."

Avi gestured behind him. "OK, well, I came over to tell you that some of the counselors are getting a photo by the sign at the entrance. Want to come?"

I looked where he had pointed and saw several others walking in that direction.

"Oh, yeah, sure. Thanks for letting me know." I walked past him and headed that way quickly so we wouldn't have to walk together.

When I approached the large wooden sign with "Camp Laurelwood" carved into it, several counselors were already huddled around. I found a spot behind the sign and crouched down to join. Avi jogged up and found a space behind me, and I felt his arm leaning on my back as someone pulled out a camera to take the photo. My cheeks blushed slightly at his touch. I was still so attracted to him in spite of myself, even though he had hurt me. Although I was looking forward to not having to see him every day, I knew a small part of me would miss those mischievous eyes and ever-illuminated smile, and those early days of the summer when we had started to connect and everything was possible. I had never met anyone like him before, and I was still dejected about how it had ended. But I smiled for the photo now, not revealing any of these emotions on my face. *Click.*

After the picture was taken, the group disassembled. As I turned to walk away, I ended up right next to Avi, and I saw that he was looking at me. His chin was angled down as he peered out at me, his eyebrows arched and his eyes questioning and apprehensive. He held out both arms tentatively.

"So, this is goodbye?"

I gave him a small, hesitant smile in return. "I guess so."

We hugged, and I deliberately wrapped my arms loosely around him so that our bodies were not otherwise touching. *What do I say to the guy that hurt me before we never see each other again?*

"Well, bye," I mustered. "It was great meeting you."

We had pulled apart now, and I saw that he was still looking at me, his eyes now a mixture of curiosity and amusement. "Bye, Jess."

I LAY LOOKING OUT AT THE WATER FROM A chaise lounge chair on the dock of my family's lake house in Pennsylvania. Summer was nearing its end, and I was back home for a couple of weeks before moving to New

York to start my sophomore year. The shiny black surface of the lake in front of me reflected the multicolored row of houses on the shore across, the image periodically scattered by a small motorboat cutting through the water. I stretched my arms up above me, realizing that after falling asleep, I had probably been in the sun a bit too long. I slowly pulled myself up out of the chair then made my way up the grassy incline of the yard and into our cottage.

I set my things down on a chair at our round kitchen table, then my older brother Steve, home from college for the time being, stopped me.

"Hey Jess, someone called for you while you were outside, but Mom thought you were sleeping."

I raised my eyebrows as I looked at him.

"Some guy named . . . Jared?" he continued. "He wanted you to call him back. He said you have his number."

Jared. We had not had any form of communication at all since the Fourth of July. I had been working under the assumption that he must have gained a sense about where I was coming from after our night at the fireworks. Over a month had passed now, and I had hoped that had provided an opportunity for both of us to start to move on. I wasn't in a hurry to call him back—I had no idea what I would say. I felt annoyed that he had even called because that indicated that we were not on the same page.

"OK, thanks," I said to my brother, who had started to walk away but then turned back and looked at me, shaking his head.

"He sounded like a real prick."

CHAPTER SEVEN

The Boy with the Guitar

I SAT AT MY WOODEN DORM ROOM DESK, MY black laptop open in front of me as I browsed through the messages in my new NYU email account. It was early September 2002, and I had recently settled into my new home in Chinatown as a sophomore, in a small suite that I shared with three other transfer students. When my parents had dropped me off, as the first one to move into our suite, I had experienced an initial moment of shock when I looked out the window and realized that I was entirely alone in New York City. But, I had since gotten more comfortable and made some friends, and classes had begun.

As I sifted through my emails, an instant message suddenly popped up in the center of the screen.

Gr8tefulDd1023: Hi there

I sighed deeply. I had not been in touch with Jared since arriving at school, and I never returned his call from when I had gotten back from camp. It had been months now since we had connected at all, and in my mind, we had both moved on. After waiting a few minutes, I realized I should probably respond.

> **JeSslcA148:** Hey
> **Gr8tefulDd1023:** How's school? All settled in?

I took my time before each reply.

> **JeSslcA148:** It's good
> **Gr8tefulDd1023:** Glad to hear it. Can't wait to hear more details.
> **Gr8tefulDd1023:** Been meaning to tell you... did you know you look like Norah Jones?
> **JeSslcA148:** Who is that?

Jared sent me a link. I clicked it, curious. A page opened up with a short article, and at the top I saw a photo of a woman who looked about my age, sitting at a piano at an angle that showed most of her face. She had long, dark, wavy hair, dark eyes, and full lips; I could see the slight resemblance in the darkness of her features and the layout of her face.

> **JeSslcA148:** I guess I can see it a little bit.
> **JeSslcA148:** That's a compliment, though - she's pretty!

Gr8tefulDd1023: Well, you're pretty =)

I exhaled again. *No. Don't flirt with me.* I had been assuming that Jared and I were on the same page about not moving forward romantically, but in an instant, I realized we had never actually had a conversation to that effect. Coming more from a place of annoyance at the fact that he was acting as though nothing had changed than from a sense of caring about his feelings, I realized that I had to say something to ensure that we shared an understanding. I took another deep breath.

JeSslcA148: Thanks!

I waited a few more moments, formulating the words. It was time. I had to tear off the Band-Aid. I put my hands back on the keyboard and typed.

JeSslcA148: So, by the way...
Gr8tefulDd1023: Yes?
JeSslcA148: I just want to make sure you know that I am not interested in anything happening between us at this point.
Gr8tefulDd1023: Okay. That was abrupt.

A minute or two passed. I had said it, and I felt my heart pumping a bit faster now. I knew I couldn't have him thinking that I somehow still liked him when that didn't feel like the case for me anymore. I wasn't sure what else to say, so I simply clicked the "x" to make the message window go away and then clicked back into my email, mindlessly scrolling. Eventually, his IM window popped back up in front of my email.

> **Gr8tefulDd1023:** Well I'll admit I'm disappointed.
> **Gr8tefulDd1023:** Are we still friends at least?

I sighed, looking past my computer as I studied the wood grain on the attached bookshelves in front of me. *Friends.* That was how we had started. If I told him we were still friends, wouldn't he just want to keep talking to me like he did before? Something had to change. I had to break away.

> **JeSslcA148:** Sure. But maybe it's best to take some time with that and just see how it goes.

If I had closed a door with my previous messages, I had just turned the key in the lock, preventing entry from the other side. Another minute passed.

> **Gr8tefulDd1023:** Okay. I understand.
> **Gr8tefulDd1023:** Bye, Jessica.

If I had closed the door and locked it, then he had just let go of the handle from the other side and walked away. I took another deep breath, my heart still pounding. I felt relieved. Ever since I saw Jared in New York that first time after our freshman year ended, I had felt unsure about what would happen with us. I had worried and wondered about why I felt the way I did, and went back and forth about it in my mind. Now, it felt like I had cast aside a weight I had been carrying that I wasn't even fully aware of.

Finally, he knew what was going on from my end. I could tell that he was angry, and I suppose he had a right to be. I knew I hadn't handled the situation all that delicately; I had merely done what I needed to do to not feel as though he was expecting something from me that I knew I could not give.

I reread Jared's words: "That was abrupt," and I knew he was right. In one moment, we were traveling through life together, sharing a small boat in a vast ocean, making our way on the journey side by side, small waves forming and breaking all around us. Quickly and unexpectedly, I jumped overboard and swam away, deciding to make it on my own while he was left alone in the boat, staring at the place where I used to sit and marveling at how swiftly our dynamic had changed.

I looked at the last message from him in the IM window still open in front of me. "Bye, Jessica." The words were so final. With a small pang, I thought back to the many late night conversations we had during our freshman year and all of the excitement and high hopes of that time. It felt a bit sad now that it had to end this way, but I knew I couldn't string him along anymore. I put my hands back on the keys to reply.

JeSslcA148: Bye, Jared

I quickly clicked the "x" to make the message window disappear, then glanced at my Buddy List in the upper righthand corner of the screen just in time to see his name switch to italics as he signed offline.

––––––

I STOOD AT THE CORNER OF WAVERLY PLACE and Broadway, my chin buried in the black scarf looped around my neck and my hands burrowed into my pockets. The January air was significantly cooler now since the sun had set, and I wished I had a hat. As I waited for the NYU shuttle bus to pull up at the corner so I could climb in for a ride back to my dorm in Chinatown, I looked around and remembered standing in the same place weeks before and meeting Ben.

Waiting with my backpack on, I had noticed him looking at me from a few yards away. I thought I recognized him from somewhere, and he was clearly an NYU student, so I walked up to face him.

"Hi! I'm Jessica. You look familiar. Do I know you from somewhere?"

He had given me a confused but pleasant smile.

"Hi, I'm not sure . . . I'm Ben."

We ended up talking until the shuttle pulled up, then we sat down next to each other in the two seats that made up a row, Ben by the window and me to his left. The seats were close together, so his black wool coat was pressed against my arm. As I periodically turned to look at him while he talked, I hadn't been able to hold back a smile as I saw him more clearly under the bright lights of the bus. He was handsome and boyish-looking with light brown hair, light hazel eyes, and a pronounced but soft nose punctuated with a well-placed mole just above his lips on the left side. He was warm and kind, and he seemed to be taking a genuine interest in what I was saying. Talking to him had felt like sitting next to a glowing campfire and toasting marshmallows on an otherwise chilly night, in an otherwise cold city, during an otherwise frigid month. It felt like I had come home to a place that I hadn't even known existed. I looked down at my legs and was glad I had gotten dressed up slightly that day with heeled black boots and my curly hair styled down around my shoulders. That shuttle ride home had been so different from every other time I rode back to my dorm in the evening when I would sit quietly alone and look out the window with everyone around me plugged into headphones.

I blinked away the memory now and craned my neck to see if I could spot the purple trolley-style bus making its way through the traffic on Broadway. I just wanted to get home and out of the cold to shed my coat, drop my bag, and throw on sweats and cozy socks in the comfort of my dorm room. I sighed, remembering what happened after that night I had met Ben on the trolley, the scenes replaying in my mind like a montage. I pictured us scrawling each other's phone numbers on scraps of paper before we parted ways when we returned to our dorm, and then I remembered him calling me on the landline phone on my desk a couple days later. That weekend we went on a date, meeting up in our lobby before walking to a coffee shop he knew about in the Village. The outside air had a chilled edge like it did tonight, and our breath had been visible in front of us as we walked together, translucent puffs of white that dissipated with each step we took, new clouds continuously forming as we talked excitedly.

I pictured us approaching the coffee shop on the corner, which had looked perfect with tiny white lights twinkling underneath the large windows, previewing a cozy and inviting ambience inside. As Ben held the door open for me in his black, thigh-length wool coat, I wondered how I had gotten so lucky. We spent the next couple hours sitting in plush fabric chairs on either side of a low table, laughing as we sipped from large white mugs of steaming hot chai lattes. It was a perfect night.

My mind flashed next to the dorm lobby, where later that night we had giggled and pointed out the cute gingerbread men cut from brown construction paper, strung up and lining the hallways as part of a holiday display. We joked about stealing one because they were so adorable. I felt my heart sink now as I recalled the empty silence in the days after our date when I didn't hear from him. Desperate for some sort of contact, I convinced someone taller than me to pull down one of the construction paper gingerbread men, and then I had gingerly carried it back to my dorm room to scrawl on it with a perfect sweet-but-casual note to Ben. I remembered knocking on his door before leaving my gift with one of his suitemates. Days later, despairing from having still not heard from him despite the note, I rode the elevator back down to his floor, and taking matters into my own hands, knocked on his door again. I couldn't let another day go by without knowing whether or not the exquisiteness that I had felt the night we went out was something I would be able to experience again.

When Ben answered dressed in sweats, he didn't invite me in. He simply told me through the doorway that he was sorry, but he wasn't interested in going out again. I pictured myself shaking slightly as I retreated down the hallway back to the elevator and sadly riding back up to my suite, having confirmed what I had already known on some level to be true. *I guess this is what rejection feels like.*

Now, I saw the orange headlights of the trolley pulling up to the street corner, snapping me out of my reverie. As I stepped inside, I didn't have an exciting conversation with a handsome stranger keeping me warm this time; I had only myself, my face buried in my scarf, on a quiet, brittle New York night. As the trolley pulled away from the curb, I looked out the window at the buildings passing by. *It's strange how so many people live here, so close together, but it can still feel so lonely.* As I watched a bodega worker pull down a metal security shutter to close up his shop for the night, I suddenly longed for connection. I had made new friends at school, but it was emotional intimacy that I craved.

By the time I was back in my dorm room, now comfortable in sweats and sitting in front of my laptop, I thought of Jared and wondered what he was up to. *Does he miss me?* I hungered for the comfortable bond we had always had over AIM. It was a cold night, and I was looking for a campfire. I signed in to AIM and scanned my Buddy List. He was still on there—Gr8tefulDd1023. And he was online. *He said he wanted to be friends at some point. Isn't now as good a time as any?* Before I could change my mind, I double clicked his name to open a new chat window.

> **JeSslcA148:** Hey!

He replied immediately.

> **Gr8tefulDd1023:** Hey! How are ya?
> **JeSslcA148:** Good! How about you?
> **Gr8tefulDd1023:** I'm good. Have a
> girlfriend now. =)

What? Did I not break things off with him like five minutes ago?

> **JeSslcA148:** Wow, nice! Good for you.
> **Gr8tefulDd1023:** Yeah...it's serious. Her
> name is Rachel.

Rachel. My mind went back to Jared's house in Queens, when I had gone to see him right after the end of our freshman year. We had been sitting in his family room, getting ready to catch the subway and wander

Manhattan, when a girl had called him. "Rachel, a friend from school," he had said.

> **Gr8tefulDd1023:** We hung out a bit last year. Actually, she's the one that gave me mono last summer ;-)
> **JeSslcA148:** Oh! Ok...

Ew.

> **Gr8tefulDd1023:** Yeah, when you and I started talking more, I sort of broke it off with her. But in the last couple months, we started talking again and now we're together.
> **Gr8tefulDd1023:** It somehow got serious pretty quickly.

Well that was quick. When Jared and I had rode together in a small boat at sea, the water representing the course of our lives, and I had without warning dove in and swam away, he may have looked wistfully at my former seat for a moment, but it wasn't for long. In the next instant, he stood up, put his hands over his eyes to block out the sun and peered out at sea. When he spotted Rachel treading water nearby, he quickly grabbed her arms and pulled her up out of the deep and into the boat where she was relieved to take the seat where I used to sit. And now, Jared and Rachel were riding the waves together; the two of them against the world. I had been replaced.

I thought of how I had felt about Jared at the end of our freshman year, how important a part of my life he had been. I had been eagerly looking forward to seeing him and discovering what we might become. Then I thought of how he, at the same time that we were talking, was seeing enough of Rachel that he caught mono from her, mono that almost kept him from visiting me in Pennsylvania that time. I felt a deep sense of unease in my gut as I realized that he had been trying to date both of us at the same time. When Jared and I had confided in each other over AIM during that transitional moment in my life, I had truly thought that we were inhabiting a special place, a world that existed only for us. Little did I know that he had other logs in the fire that had been providing my heat.

Talking to Jared now, the tone of our IMs had clearly changed. The warm closeness that I had been seeking was nowhere to be found. I knew it wasn't fair, but I resented the fact that he was now with someone else since it meant that the tenor of our conversation had shifted. I needed the old Jared in this moment, but he wasn't available to me. My experience with Ben had been the first time my hopes had been dashed so drastically by something I had believed to be that promising, and it had set me adrift. I had a chill, and I was seeking out a campfire at a campsite where someone else had already set up for the night.

———

I LEANED AGAINST THE WALL NEXT TO THE metal door of my dorm suite, my legs covered in gray sweatpants and bent in front of me. The floor tile beneath me was so cold it touched the soles of my feet, making a mockery of my white socks. I was grateful to have found a place that I could have phone conversations with some degree of privacy away from my three suitemates, even if the conditions weren't perfectly temperate.

I looked at the black cordless landline phone in my right hand then down at the bright pink Post-it Note stuffed in the palm of my left hand where I had scrawled Jared's new dorm number. We had made a plan to catch up on the phone, an effort on my part to recreate some of our past rapport. As I dialed the number and listened to it ring on the other end, I thought about how much had changed since we had last spoken on the phone. *Will it be the same?*

After Jared picked up, we spent a few minutes catching up. I was excited to tell him about what I was studying at NYU.

"Right now I'm taking intermediate Spanish and also intensive beginners French. I'm thinking about majoring in Romance Languages, French and Spanish."

Jared gushed in response, "That's really great, Jess. Why not just dive in, right?"

I went on, "Yeah, I would just have to choose where I'd study abroad—it would either be Paris or Madrid since NYU has programs in both places . . . but I don't think I could swing both . . . or maybe I could . . ."

As he told me about his own plans to travel abroad somewhere Spanish-speaking, it felt exciting to impart my dreams to him, given our shared love for travel and exploration. There was so much more I wanted to tell him about life in New York and about my plans at school, but he suddenly interrupted me.

"Jess, it's so great to catch up, but I actually have to run. Rachel just got here and we're headed out."

My heart sank. "Oh, OK, no problem. We'll talk more another time."

I felt ill at ease as I clicked the "Off" button on the cordless phone and stared down at the large square tiles making up the institutional-looking hallway floor that now somehow felt even colder. It bothered me that I couldn't have Jared's full attention. It was divided, shared with Rachel. I knew it wasn't warranted—I had willingly broken things off with him. But I thirsted for the easy dynamic we had had before. It had already become clear to me that it was not easy to meet people in general at NYU, and even more difficult to find people I might be interested in dating. I couldn't help but wonder if I had missed my chance with Jared. *Did I have real feelings for him and push him away?* Now I was afraid that I would never get the chance to find out.

———

I STEPPED ONTO THE CROSSWALK ON CANAL Street just as the white figure lit up on the walk sign. *Two more blocks.* I clutched both straps of my black backpack, ducking my head against the cold mist that didn't seem to be falling in a downward motion but instead almost coming up from the ground somehow. It was another chilly February day in New York, and I couldn't wait to get back to the toasty embrace of my dorm room and to kick off my shoes.

Finally, I crossed the last side street and approached my dorm on the right. I lifted my head up to grab the door handle then suddenly noticed a guy standing just to the right of the entrance, smoking. I looked at him with surprise—it was such an oppressively dreary day to be outside. I had seen this guy around the building before. He was always wearing a well-worn, faded blue jean jacket with various colorful patches sewn onto it, including a large black and white peace sign that stood out against the broken-in denim. His skin was fair, and his curly black hair was unruly around his head like a thick cloud of dark smoke. He wore glasses and had an air about him that was equal parts edgy and sensitive. We had crossed paths before at this same spot, but we never spoke to each other.

As I reached for the door handle, anxious to get to the heat beckoning from inside, I shot another quick sidelong glance in his direction and accidentally caught his eye. *Oops. Am I supposed to say hi?* I had resolutely cloaked myself in my stone-faced, unapproachable city mode for the last twenty minutes as I briskly walked home from class, and as our eyes met now, I was instantly caught off guard by making even the slightest connection with another human being. I didn't think I could rein in my momentum to get inside if I tried, so I simply gave him a half smile as he exhaled cigarette smoke into the chilly New York air, and then the interior glass double doors closed behind me. Once inside, I glanced back over my right shoulder at him through the glass. He was still standing there, one leg propped up against the building. *He must really want to smoke.* But I could also tell that despite the cold, he seemed to simply enjoy being outside where he could watch everyone arrive back home for the evening, like a doorman. He wasn't in a hurry to be anywhere or to do anything in particular, which stood in stark contrast to my own kinetic energy propelling me home.

———

"SO HOW'S NYU?" LISA ASKED AS I LEANED against the wall to my suite, my black cordless phone pressed against my right ear and my legs crossed in front of me on the hallway floor.

"It's good," I told her, then gave an overview of my various classes and some of the people I had met before we quickly devolved into reminiscence of high school inside jokes that we still found hilarious.

All of a sudden, I heard the delicate strumming of acoustic guitar chords from nearby, resonating in the long dorm hallway. Lisa was telling me a story now, but as she did I leaned forward and used my other ear to try and determine where this pleasant sound was coming from. It seemed to be originating from around the corner on the same floor as me. As I heard a male voice begin to sing softly with the guitar, I briefly moved the phone away from my ear and craned my head to get a better listen. The voice was unexpectedly beautiful, like a delicate stream weaving its way around the concrete and steel of the city.

"So there's this guy singing on my floor," I finally said to Lisa. "I'm going to go see where it's coming from; hold on a second."

I pried myself up from the cold tile floor and carried the cordless phone with me as I took a few quiet steps down the hall toward where the music was coming from. I was pulled in by the voice like a siren song and was instantly transported somewhere far from my otherwise ordinary Sunday night in the hallway outside my room to a place that was calmer, more open, and more comfortable somehow. I couldn't stop listening—I didn't want to leave this newfound habitat. As I approached the corner and heard the voice more loudly, I realized it was now just next to me. When I slowly peeked my head around the corner, still clutching the cordless phone, I immediately recognized the cloud of black curly hair, the glasses, and the faded jean jacket with the colored patches. He was sitting on the other side of the hallway from me, leaning against the wall as he held the large acoustic guitar, his legs outstretched in front of him. The caramel-colored wood of his instrument shone under the flourescent lights.

He didn't look up, and I didn't want to make my presence known, so I quickly pulled myself back around the corner. I stood still for a few more moments as I listened to his soothing voice along with the pleasant strums of his guitar. His words carried the weight of emotion but were also restrained; in them I could hear that there was so much more that he wanted to say, things that he wanted to share with the world. But he sang softly, gently, unhurried.

I smiled to myself as I tiptoed in my socks back toward my dorm suite with Lisa still waiting on the other end of the line. I loved how the dark-haired guy who usually smoked out front had so comfortably planted himself in the hallway outside his room like I had done. I didn't usually see anyone in these cold and quiet corridors unless they were on their way to or from somewhere. I particularly enjoyed the fact that he had his guitar with him, too, as if the hallway were an extension of his own living room. For a moment, seeing and hearing him somehow personalized this large building where I didn't know that many people, and the whole place felt a bit cozier.

When I was back by the door to my suite, I turned around and slid down the wall, planting myself on the floor again. "Hey, are you still there?" I said into the phone.

Lisa giggled. "Yep! What's going on?"

"So yeah, there's this guy sitting in the hall singing with his guitar," I continued. "But he's really good. I wish you could hear it. I actually feel like this guy would be your type—skinny, pale, and artsy."

Lisa laughed. "I'm jealous. Why can't I find someone skinny, pale, and artsy playing guitar in my dorm?"

———

I NEEDED TWO HANDS TO HEAVE MY BULGING mesh laundry bag over the threshold before the metal dorm suite door slammed behind me. It was Sunday—laundry day. I trudged down the hallway, mostly dragging the colossal bag that I could barely keep off the ground as I made my way around the corner toward the shared laundry room.

"Oh!" I said with surprise as I looked down to see a bespectacled face with a haze of dark curly hair glance up at me.

He was sitting in the same place I had seen him a few weeks before, on the floor against the wall, with his guitar on his lap. He must not have been playing yet, because I had no idea he was there until we were face to face.

As our eyes met, I gave him a small smile, then all at once I felt embarrassed, remembering that I was wearing an old sweatshirt and sweatpants with my hair haphazardly pulled back behind me, and no trace of makeup or jewelry to be found. Aware of the multitude of dirty underwear likely visible through the small holes in the mammoth bag I toted behind me, I quickly opened the laundry room door, heaved the bag in, then disappeared inside as the door closed behind me.

After throwing my clothes into the washing machine, I hurried back to my room with little acknowledgement of the guy outside in the hallway, so later, when I left my room again to switch my clothes to the dryer, I was pleased to hear his voice singing softly from around the corner. This time I was prepared. I had taken off my oversized and unflattering hoodie and was wearing a more fitted T-shirt with my sweatpants, and I had even looked in the mirror to apply some lip gloss and confirm my hair was in place. As I turned the corner and approached him, this time the sound of his soft voice melting against the rich acoustic chords was so spellbinding that I actually stopped in front of him in spite of myself, just to listen. He looked up when he saw me, and his contemplative expression broke into a small smile, his dark eyebrows raised slightly for a moment. He continued to play, and I remained standing there, frozen in time and space, watching and listening. I was rooted in place, but his voice moved me. I couldn't sit down—that would have been making myself way too comfortable; I didn't even know this guy. We'd never even spoken, so I couldn't just invite myself into his extended living room. But I simply had to keep listening, so I didn't move.

I continued to stand there, fixated, as he began a new song with lyrics about a sun rising and setting. When he finished singing and strummed the last chord, he stopped and looked up at me in the silence.

"That one was about George W. He's the 'son' in the song."

Nice. I finally mustered, "You're so good. I love just a voice with an acoustic guitar. It's my favorite."

He smiled gently as he looked at me. "Thanks." He looked back down again and began to aimlessly strum on the strings.

"I'm Jessica by the way."

He lifted a hand up from the guitar and stretched it out to me. "Sam."

I shook his hand then suddenly felt awkward when I realized how long I had been standing there. I shot my eyes toward the laundry room door.

"Well, I gotta grab my laundry. But you should keep playing. It sounds so good."

Sam smiled up at me again. "Thanks. It's nice to meet you, Jessica."

I grinned as I pushed open the door to the laundry room. *He's cute.* Beyond that, what was even more attractive to me was his evident passion. It was clear that he felt a lot of things, including angst about the state of the world, and was compelled to make music as a result so he could share his message. But there was no anger in his singing, only gentleness. What I liked best, though, was that while he was undeniably very talented, he wasn't playing softly in the hallway to impress anyone. He simply wanted a quiet place to sing and strum on his guitar where there was space to do so. I could completely relate to his instinct to seek out a more private sanctuary from the cacophony of roommate and dorm room sounds.

———

A FEW DAYS LATER, AS I WALKED QUICKLY UP to my dorm building, returning from class on a cool March day, I saw Sam standing outside the entrance with a cigarette. This time, I gave him a familiar smile.

"Hey," we both said to each other.

It was nice to now feel connected to this guy who I saw all the time, and I appreciated having another association in this otherwise impersonal building, in an otherwise detached city. I was glad he couldn't see the smile I was unable to hide as the heavy glass doors closed behind me and I headed toward the elevators.

————

IT WAS FINALLY STARTING TO FEEL LIKE SPRING outside. The briskness of March had given way to some sunny April days, and yellow daffodils and pink and white tulips had begun to spring up around the trees in the small metal squares that ran along the sidewalks. It was another Sunday night, and I was, predictably, doing my laundry. As I again dragged my awkwardly overfilled laundry bag through the door of my dorm suite and across the cold tiled hallway floor, I actively hoped I might see Sam on my way. As the suite door closed behind me, I felt a warm comfort melt over me when I heard gentle guitar strumming from around the corner. I made my way down the hallway, and when I turned the corner, I made sure to carefully lift my bag around Sam's legs, which were again outstretched in front of him on the floor. When I looked down, I noticed that he was wearing fuzzy navy blue and burgundy printed socks and no shoes. I smiled, again appreciating how easily Sam made the hallway of this cold dorm, in a city of anonymous faces, simply an extension of his own living space. It was evident to me that he was someone who made it a point to step outside norms in order to call them into question.

"Hey," I said, still smiling.

Sam looked up and met my grin with his own. "Laundry time?"

"Indeed." I pointed down at his guitar. "That sounds great."

I went into the laundry room and began to separate out my darks and lights, with the door kept slightly propped open by my laundry bag. I heard the sound of new chords as Sam started to play a different song. As I listened, I could tell that this was one I hadn't heard him play before. He hit the pretty chords slowly and slightly apprehensively, as though this was one of the first times he had played them and he was still figuring out how he wanted the song to sound. I tossed a pile of darks into the washing machine, poured in some detergent, and pressed start just as he began to sing. I walked back out into the hallway then, in time to stop and listen.

Sam's head was bent down as he played.

"I see her . . . she sees me, I'm wondering where she's got to be. . . ." He turned his head up and peeked at me before looking back down at the guitar. He came to the refrain now. "So why don't you . . . take off your shoes. . . ." He met my eyes again for a quick flash.

It feels like he's singing to me. As his soothing voice and melodic playing melded together and coated the air with the warmth of a chunky cable knit sweater, I again felt locked into place, yet at the same time transported from where I stood. I was no longer in the bland hallways of our dorm on Sunday night, thinking about the next day's classes; instead, I was carried into the glow of this new, comfortable space with Sam. I was content here, and I felt like a purer version of myself in this place. I didn't want to leave. Eventually, though, Sam finished the song, and the hallway was quiet again.

He smiled modestly. "That's one of my new ones."

"I love it," I said simply, still looking at him.

I didn't want to linger there for too much longer, so I tore myself away and headed back toward my suite. As I walked, I could hear Sam strumming lightly while quietly singing the chorus again: "So why don't you . . . take off your shoes. . . ."

I thought about how it had felt like he was singing to me moments before. I looked down at the gym sneakers I had tied on to get to the laundry room, then thought about the fuzzy socks I had seen on Sam's feet. Then I remembered all of those times that I had hurried past him outside of our dorm building as he stood there smoking in the cold, how we always saw each other, but never spoke. "So why don't you . . . take off your shoes. . . ." *Is he singing about me?* I shook my head, trying to rid my mind of a possibility that seemed too remote.

I ZIPPED CLOSED A LARGE RED DUFFLE BAG that was filled to the brim with folded clothes. Sophomore year had ended. My final exams were completed and two of my suite mates had already moved out. The one remaining still had some of her things in the other bedroom, but she was out at the moment, so I had the suite to myself at this midday hour. As I packed up the last of my things, I thought about the people and the dorm that I would be leaving behind for the summer. I remembered Sam and realized I wouldn't see him standing out front of our building anymore, cigarette in hand. I thought about his soft voice and the delicate guitar chords, how they had entranced me on so many otherwise ordinary Sunday nights, and I was suddenly wistful for those moments. *Maybe we can stay in touch.* The school year was over, but maybe the music didn't have to stop. I wondered whether he had moved out of the building yet.

I remembered back to the night when it had felt like Sam was singing to me. I thought for a moment, staring at my red bag in the center of the floor, then decided that he might want to stay in touch with me, too. Running with that feeling, and moving quickly before I talked myself out of it, I grabbed a pad of bright blue Post-it Notes and a pen from among the few items remaining on my desk. Hurriedly, I jotted down my name with my NYU email address below it. I carefully tore off another Post-it and affixed it to the back of the first to remove the stickiness, and then took a deep breath and walked out of my suite and into the hallway.

After I turned the corner, I looked down at the spot where I had seen Sam play his guitar all of those times and felt my chest warm from the comfort of the memory. I fixed my eyes on the metal door to his suite, took another deep breath, then knocked and waited. I felt my heart rate accelerate as I realized how little interaction Sam and I had actually had. I had never knocked on his door before, and I had never been inside his suite; I didn't even know who he lived with. I also didn't know whether he was still in there, or if he had already packed up his things and left his sophomore year behind him, leaving me with nothing more than the memory of the sound of his voice outside the laundry room. I stood staring at the door. *Maybe he's already gone.* I exhaled again and gave one more firm knock, just in case, then waited.

Suddenly I heard heavy footsteps plodding toward the door. *Someone's there.* A moment later, the door opened up, just a several inch-wide crack. I saw Sam on the other side, his dark curly hair rumpled, and his eyes squinty with sleep. *Crap, I woke him up.*

"Hey," I said quickly, and stuck the Post-it through the opening. "I just wanted to give you my email so we could stay in touch."

He blinked a few times, wearily processing what I had said, then looked at the piece of paper. "Oh yeah, OK, cool. Thanks."

His voice was sleepy and surprised, but not unfriendly.

"Take care," he said, and the door closed.

I walked back down the hall to my suite feeling slightly embarrassed for having made such a daring move. Maybe I had imagined any connection Sam and I might have had. He hadn't ever gone out of his way to track me down, outside of the hallway by the laundry room, away from the front doors of our building. But, I simply knew that if there was anything I could do to give myself an opportunity to hear him play again—to keep the music going—then I had to do it. And, if by chance he was singing about me that night, maybe I needed to act to demonstrate to him that his message had been received. Also, I just had a sense that I needed to keep the door open—even just a crack—because our story wasn't done yet; for some reason it felt like I was supposed to keep knowing Sam. As the metal door to my suite closed behind me, echoing in the near emptiness, I nodded to myself, satisfied with what I had done. *Now it's up to him.* I knew at least this way, I wouldn't be left wondering without having tried to do something about it.

———

I CLIMBED DOWN OUT OF MY FAMILY'S GOLD Ford Expedition and clicked the door shut behind me. Dana, a friend from high school, was having a small gathering at her place tonight, and I had just pulled into her driveway. It was the summer after my sophomore year, and I was spending it living at home in Pennsylvania, working as a server at a restaurant in the Scranton mall. Occasionally after I finished a shift, I would stay in the area and hang out with friends before driving the dark, winding streets back to our lake cottage to sleep at night.

I pulled on my jean jacket now to cover up my pink polo shirt from work, then opened the door and entered the kitchen to see Dana and several other friends surrounding the kitchen island.

"Hey!" I said, setting my purse down on a barstool.

As I looked around, my curly hair clipped up behind my head, I paused with surprise when I saw a tall figure standing to my left. I hadn't noticed him at first. A casual white button-down shirt in a material that looked soft. Jeans. Narrow, handsome features with short, dark blond hair spiked up around his head with gel. Rob Kowalski. I smiled at him. *I didn't know he was coming. This gathering just got way more interesting.* Though we chatted on IM very occasionally, this may have been the first time I had seen him since we graduated high school two years before.

I felt myself blushing now as I was taken back to 1996 when I first met Rob, when we were both thirteen on the dance floor at a Bat Mitzvah party in a hotel banquet room. I had stood with a small circle of girls as the Spice Girls' "Wannabe" blared from the tall speakers on either side of the DJ booth, bopping happily in my white strappy shoes with tall, chunky heels, pale green and purple flowered Gap skirt, and a matching light green sweater. As the final notes of the song played, I felt something touch my head, and I looked up with surprise to see that someone had tapped me with the skinny end of an inflatable guitar, one of the many party props that the DJ had handed out to the crowd. My eyes traced the neon green and black vinyl back to a face several yards and multiple dancing teenagers away from me. Rob Kowalski. He was tall and lanky with brown eyes and neat, dark blond hair parted down the middle. We weren't friends; I knew that he played trumpet in the school band like I did, but he didn't sit in my row. He was also in a band that had played in the middle school talent show recently, so everyone knew who he was. We shared some mutual friends, but I didn't think we had ever spoken. By the time I met his eyes, everyone around us had started bouncing gleefully to Jamiroquai's "Virtual Insanity." He didn't even say anything to me as he retreated his inflatable guitar, he just looked at me steadily with his dark, confident eyes and the tiniest hint of a smile on his lips. I felt my face flush a hot red as an ebullient excitement began to course through my veins. It had been just the slightest of actions, but in tapping my head from afar it felt like Rob had anointed me as the object of his affection. I had been chosen, somehow, among all of the other seventh grade girls who had crushes on him since his band played on stage.

When I saw Rob at the next bat mitzvah on the circuit a few weeks later, we deliberately sat in rows near each other, and an understanding was soon reached that we were "going out." This meant little beyond in name only, never included physically going to any place, and reached its finale a few weeks later when I heard in the cafeteria that he planned to dump me, so I sauntered up to him and did it first. I don't think we ever even had a full conversation during the entire several-week-long relationship.

As I looked at him now, I remembered the last time I had seen him. It was on another dance floor, this time a makeshift one, at an awkward party in our high school cafeteria right after we had all graduated. I had been holding the hands of a male friend of mine as we laughed and danced together dramatically when Rob suddenly appeared and jokingly asked if he could cut in. We never really talked to each other, so it had been surprising to see him. These were supposed to be the final moments that we all had together though, the last chance to do or say something before we all went our separate ways into adulthood. I felt hope in my chest as Rob stood next to us, his demeanor flirtatious. For the briefest moment my eyes met his, and I saw a flash of interest and intrigue mixed in with his jesting expression, as though he did indeed want to dance with me. Before I had the chance to figure it out, though, he was gone.

And now here we were, in Dana's kitchen two years later. We were college students now, and things felt different, but as I felt my face light up, the heat on my cheeks and the excitement in my chest were the same as when I was barely a teenager and I noticed him for the first time on the dance floor.

He sauntered over to the small table in the corner where I was pouring myself a cup of Diet Coke. "What are YOU drinking, Jessica?" He asked, eyeing my clear plastic cup. "Can I add some rum to your coke? I've got the good stuff over here." He gestured to a half empty bottle of amber liquid resting on the kitchen island.

I shook my head. "Looks yummy, but I'm driving. I'm a lightweight, so I've learned it's better to just not mix the two at all."

He playfully scoffed. "A lightweight, eh? Laaaame."

He stood over me and studied my face, and I felt his gaze on my lips. My face flushed warm again, and I instinctively looked away toward the others. *Did we just have a moment?*

"Alright, well, I for one do need more rum," Rob said suddenly, and then he made his way back toward the other side of the kitchen.

I exhaled and joined the group at the island, unable to suppress the small smile on my face. It was exciting to have someone to flirt with in our quiet hometown in the summertime.

———————

A FEW WEEKS LATER I FOUND MYSELF IN DA-na's house again; she had thrown a party while her parents were out of town. As I made my way into her living room with a red solo cup of seltzer, I could hear Matchbox Twenty playing from the stereo. I scanned the group, then my stom-ach did some small flips when I caught sight of Rob. He looked casually cool in jeans, a tight white T-shirt that accen-tuated his muscular arms, and his hair gelled upward. When I had seen him at Dana's the last time, I had come straight from work and probably reeked of French fries, but tonight I had been able to put some effort in. I felt smart in my flared jeans, black sleeveless shirt with a small colorful design, black wedge flip flops, and some light but carefully applied makeup.

Soon he was in front of me.

"Hey Jessica."

I smiled up at him as I cradled my red cup. "Hey, what's going on?"

He's definitely gotten cuter. And is way more built than I remembered.

"Oh, you know, the usual," he said with a smile. "Hanging out, causing trouble."

I felt my face warm as he spoke; he was standing so close to me. *Maybe now is our chance.* I watched him take a several-gulp long swig from the beer bottle in his hand. *OK, someone already had a few before I got here. . . .*

A little while later as I stood chatting with Dana and a few girlfriends, I was aware of Rob standing in the small circle just next to mine, his back to the wall. I took a small sip of seltzer. *I wish I wasn't driving.* Suddenly I heard a loud crash nearby where Rob stood. Everyone was silent for a moment and there was a pause in the general merriment as we all turned to look at Rob. He had backed into a long mirror hanging on the wall behind him, knocking it to the ground and shattering it. I watched as he stumbled away from the reflective shards confusedly. *Wow, he's even drunker than I thought.*

The girls I had been standing with all rushed toward the mess.

"What am I supposed to tell my parents?!" I could hear Dana yelling, but my attention was on Rob, who had now laid down on a brown leather couch off to the side, his eyes closed.

Jeez, is he OK? Doesn't anyone care?

I made my way over to him and crouched down in front of the couch near his head. I picked up a bottle of water from the glass coffee table next to him, twisted it open, and held it out to him. "Hey, is this yours? You should really have some water."

He opened his brown eyes and looked at me. "Everything is just . . . spinning. . . ." he said before closing his eyes again.

I sighed. "Yeah. This will help."

He peeked at the bottle then took it from my hand and pulled himself up to take a small sip before lying right back down and shutting his eyes once more.

I stood up then and found Dana. "Hey, should we be worried about Rob?"

Her eyes widened. "Oh, I'm so pissed at him right now. And I know. He's so drunk. We already called his brother, and he's on the way to pick him up."

I nodded, relieved. I was concerned about him. It seemed like everyone else had simply gone back to partying now while Rob lay nearly passed out on the couch.

I looked over at him then gingerly walked back toward the couch and sat down in front of it again. He was still lying on his back with his eyes closed. I studied the sharp spikes of his sandy blond-brown hair, hardened with gel around his head. *Defies gravity.* I felt my cheeks redden again as I looked at the long straight nose of his movie star-handsome profile. I sighed, embarrassed for Rob that he had broken the mirror, and now everyone was annoyed at him, and I felt the shame as if it were my own.

"Rob, you still with me? Your brother is on the way."

He squinted without opening his eyes. "Thank you, Jessica. Ah, Mitch, always coming to my rescue and pulling me out of deep shit."

I gave a small laugh and handed him the water bottle again. "Here. Drink more of this."

He sat up and took a long swig this time. Just as he went to set the bottle back down on the glass coffee table, Mitch burst into the room, his trendy khaki coat glistening with a light dusting of fresh rain drops. He approached the couch, and I quickly briefed him on Rob's condition.

"He knocked a mirror off the wall and broke it, and he's been over here ever since. He's been drinking water though."

Mitch eyed Rob then the bottle. "Good. Alright, thanks Jessica. I've got it from here."

I nodded and watched as Mitch pulled Rob up from the couch then talked to him quietly with his arm around his shoulders before they made their way out the door together.

After the door clicked shut, I looked back at the empty couch and wondered if Rob would even remember that I had sat with him. I sighed as I glanced around me. The party was in full swing again now, and Maroon Five was blasting from the stereo speakers. I wanted to have fun, but it felt like the air had left the room a bit. I picked up my red cup from the coffee table where I had left it and took another sip. I didn't even fully understand why I had felt so compelled to protect Rob, to be there for him when everyone else shunned him. We weren't even really that good of friends, but I still felt an inexplicable vibe with him that seemed to have not changed after all this time. For some reason I felt like I had an obligation to be there for him, and while I knew it was silly, it was one that I was happy to fulfill.

Maybe it was because deep underneath the new layers that had formed around me during the intervening years,

I was still the same girl he had chosen with an inflatable guitar in 1996. And he still somehow managed to give me butterflies in my stomach, even when he was drunk and nearly out cold on a couch at an underage party. I shook my head and gazed up at the door again. *Just another missed chance.*

SOON IT WAS AUGUST, AND I WAS STARTING to think about getting back to New York for my junior year. I sat down now at the desk in our family room to check my NYU email. I rolled the chair up to the keyboard and clicked into the computer, then mindlessly signed into AIM out of habit.

A few seconds later a message popped up on the screen.

DeepBlue21983: Hey Jess

Rob. We had not seen each other or communicated at all since Dana's party a few weeks before. I set my hands on the keyboard for a moment trying to figure out what to write.

JeSslcA148: Hey! How's it going?
DeepBlue21983: Not bad
DeepBlue21983: Mitch tells me you were helpful at the party the other weekend
JeSslcA148: Yeah, I guess so? I was happy to help

DeepBlue21983: Sorry you had to see that

DeepBlue21983: Not one of my finest moments

JeSslcA148: It happens, it's all good

DeepBlue21983: Yeah

I took a deep breath. *So what happens next?* I saw him send another message.

DeepBlue21983: You still up at the lake?

JeSslcA148: Yep, I'm here for two more weeks before I head back to school

Why?

DeepBlue21983: Nice. I love sailing up there.

DeepBlue21983: I'll probably get the truck out there again one of these days.

JeSslcA148: Nice! Well, I'm around.

With just enough time left to hang out . . .

DeepBlue21983: Hey I gotta run

OK, or not...

JeSslcA148: Ok, ttyl!

DeepBlue21983: Cya later

I sighed as I watched his name switch to italics in my Buddy List, and a closed door icon appeared next to it. *Missed chances are all we will ever have.*

I tapped my fingers on the desk in front of me, then remembered why I had sat down at the computer to begin with. I clicked the "x" on the corner of my IM window with Rob to make it disappear then opened up a new browser window and logged into my school email. As I scanned through the new messages, one jumped out at me—it was from someone named Samuel Isaacs. It didn't look like spam and appeared to be from another NYU account, but I didn't recognize the name. It was always nice to see an email from a real person, though, rather than one of the many mass communications I was subscribed to. "Hey," read the subject line. *Do I know this person?* Furrowing my brow, I clicked on the email to open it.

> Hey Jess,
>
> This is Sam I. You gave me your email address, so I figured I would use it. So, hey. How's your summer going? Do you know where you'll be living in the fall?
>
> Sam

I stared at the words, my head tilted slightly to the left now. *Sam?* My eyes focused in on the words "You gave me your email address." All at once my face lit up with recognition, and I felt a flutter in my stomach as I remembered that day packing up my sophomore year dorm room. I pictured the bright blue Post-it Note with my information scrawled on it, and I saw Sam's face framed with dark curly hair rumpled from sleep as he looked at me confusedly through the crack in his door. *Of course. Sam!*

I smiled now, re-reading the email. *He reached out to me.* I felt content in the knowledge that my audacious instinct to slip him my information had not been for naught, and I was delighted to hear from him. NYU felt so far removed from my experience at home, and it was nice to feel a connection to the upcoming year as the summer was nearing its end. Seeing Sam's email confirmed for me that it wasn't just I who felt compelled to stay in touch, to keep the conversation going that started outside the laundry room.

I wrote him back, and we each sent a few more emails before he suggested that we meet up once we were both back in the city. We exchanged phone numbers and AIM screen names so we could stay in touch when the semester started. I was excited to have the opportunity to get to know Sam, and connecting with him added an extra layer of adventure to the upcoming school year.

CHAPTER EIGHT

Missed Connections

I PUSHED OPEN THE GLASS DOORS OF NYU'S Third North dorm and felt the balmy air on my face. It was early September, but it still felt like summer. I had recently moved back to school into my new dorm at Third Avenue and Twelfth Street. I looked around just in time to see Sam crossing the street and approaching my corner. He wore jeans and a subtly western-looking blue and white button-up shirt and trendy red sneakers. His deep black curly hair was as I remembered it, if trimmed down slightly. *Does he remember what I look like?*

He stepped across the curb and looked directly at me, his face now broken into a wide smile.

"Hey!"

OK, phew.

"Hey!" I said, meeting his grin with my own.

I was happy to see Sam, and it was exciting to know that we were about to spend some quality time together.

Between quick hellos at the door to our building and brief chats in the hallway, our face-to-face opportunities last year had been so limited. I walked up to him now in my black sandals with a slight wedge heel, my silver chandelier-style earrings with sparkly marcasite stones dancing slightly with each step. I had endeavored to look nice enough for a date yet not too dressy for a weeknight, and in my dark jeans and black sleeveless drape neck top, I felt like I had succeeded. The dense, humid air made me feel grateful that my curly hair was already pulled back with a clip.

Standing across from Sam now, I suddenly felt slightly nervous. I had not been on that many dates since I had started school, or on that many dates, period.

He looked at me, still smiling. "So there's a great place I know on St. Marks—want to head that way?"

I felt relieved that I didn't have to come up with something.

"Sounds great!"

As we walked together on the sidewalk heading eastward, the sun was beginning to set, casting a yellow glow behind the tops of the buildings that seamlessly flowed into the still-visible gray-blue of the daytime sky. The sidewalks were lined with clusters of people enjoying this final taste of summer before the brisk fall soon set in.

I was elated to be on a date. New York was so inherently romantic to me, given its abundant opportunities for perfect dates—a seemingly endless array of cozy restaurants, a Central Park ripe for strolling, new and interesting bars always opening up and ready to be discovered, and Broadway. Being single, I sometimes felt excluded from all of the perfect couple opportunities that the city presented on a bustling silver platter. Walking along with a cute boy now, on our way to somewhere fun on an unseasonably warm night made me feel like one of the lucky ones.

After we walked for about ten minutes, Sam stopped in front of an awning-covered patio and gestured at a small stairwell leading down to an entrance. The word "YAFFA" was spelled out in small tiles above the door.

"We're here," he said. "Have you been to Yaffa Cafe before?"

I shook my head. "No, it looks great."

Sam walked down the several concrete steps and held the door open for me. I stepped inside to see colorful, eclectic decor and animal print everywhere.

"Wow!" I said. "Looks fun."

Sam smiled and led us to a table. "This is one of my favorite places."

We sat down in a booth with zebra print benches and a leopard print table. I set my bag down next to me on the bench and looked around. The lights inside were dim and the room was lit mostly by tiny brightly colored bulbs strung up around the space. The decor was so intentionally over the top that it somehow worked together aesthetically. I wasn't surprised that Sam liked it here. *Alternative with a bit of an edge, just like him.*

After a waitress approached our table and we ordered, we talked for a little while about our respective families and childhoods before quickly delving into deeper topics.

I could see that he was genuine, the kind of person that didn't make a lot of small talk just for the sake of it, which I appreciated. He was frank, honest, and just unabashedly himself as he told me about the women's studies classes that he was taking.

"I'm a lipstick feminist," he said confidently.

I gave him a puzzled look as I took a sip from my straw. "What does that mean?"

He looked at me through his glasses and explained, "For a woman, it essentially means that you can be a feminist but still wear makeup. And not wear Birkenstocks. And I support that."

I nodded, thinking I could get on board with that as well. I felt myself smiling continuously as we talked; I was having a great time. We were having one of my favorite kinds of conversations—a good, deep one where I knew I would walk away having expanded the way I thought about something.

I felt challenged by Sam, if slightly intimidated. His natural directness made me feel as though my responses to him would need to be equally as unguarded, and I wasn't completely sure I was ready to lay everything out on the leopard print table just yet. He seemed so compelling that I couldn't help but wonder if I was interesting enough for him. I took a deep breath. *Just be yourself. He's nice.*

By the time we stepped back out onto the sidewalk after our long meal, we had an easy conversational rapport going.

"It's so nice outside still," I said.

The sky was black now, but I still felt the thick warm air against my skin, its density cut slightly by a gentle breeze. It was truly a perfect night for a date.

Sam gestured eastward. "Should we keep walking for a bit?"

I nodded, and we turned and continued on together in step. As we walked side by side chatting animatedly, I started to notice that when Sam glanced over at me, his eyes would linger for a moment, his small smile unrelenting. I felt my heart rate accelerate as everything all at once felt as though it was happening too quickly. First, Sam had simply been the mysterious, intriguing guy smoking outside my dorm building every day. Then, he was the one whose amazing voice captivated me on my way to do laundry. I didn't know what exactly I wanted from him now; I had wanted to stay in touch because I had felt enough intrigue, enough of a potential connection with him that needed to be explored. So the door was opened, just a crack. And now, just like that, here we were, having a great time, and I was getting the palpable vibe that he was interested in me, but at the same time I was also becoming keenly aware that I was not equipped to deal with that.

The door had now been pushed open almost all of the way, and everything felt very real and equally frightening. This incredibly smart, cool person liked *me*? Did he even know enough about me? Was I cool enough for him? Maybe I had held my own in our conversation at the cafe and on the walk so far, but would he imminently realize that I wasn't so fascinating and that would be it? When he looked at me, I could see the emotional depth in his dark eyes, and I felt unprepared to be on the receiving end of that. Did I even have the same to give in return? I was concerned that Sam thought I liked him also, and now I felt entirely overwhelmed.

We passed by a bakery on our right with pastries in neat rows lining the large rectangular window facing the street. Our slow walk came to a halt as we instinctively stopped to gaze at the pastiche of golden brown delicacies in every shape and size, brightly illuminated by warm yellow lights shining from above. The neon letters in the window cast a pink glare onto Sam's face as he peered through the glass.

"Bear claws!!" he exclaimed with excitement, and I watched as his laid-back demeanor gave way to unbridled childlike joy as he spoke more quickly now. "So I'm from outside of Boston, and bear claws are totally a thing there. They're SO good. Should we get some?"

I glanced in the window quizzically. "What's a bear claw?"

Sam gasped and looked at me with amazement, his mouth agape. "You've never . . . had a BEAR CLAW? We're going in." He started to walk toward the door, but paused just before his hand reached the handle and turned to look back at me. "Is that OK, or do you have to get back?"

I looked back at him and blinked, my sandal-covered feet planted where they were as I felt my breath tighten. I was stuck in place on the sidewalk outside this adorable bakery with this lovely person on this wonderful night. Stuck in place, stuck in time, stuck in life. It was as though the sidewalk cement had not yet dried when I had stepped up to look in the bakery window, and now, when I tried to move, I found I was a permanent part of this patch of the East Village concrete. I didn't want to go backward, but I was too afraid to step forward. Walking inside this bakery with Sam could lead to so much more that I didn't think I was prepared for yet. I had thought I wanted to keep the music going, but the record scratched to a sudden stop—*vvvvvhhhhtttttt*—and all was quiet now as I felt a growing knot in the pit of my stomach.

"I think I better get back, actually," I said quickly. "I'm kind of tired, and there's a few things I still need to do tonight."

Sam's face fell slightly as he nodded. "Okay."

We turned to walk back in the opposite direction. I wasn't tired, and there was nothing else I had to do that night. As we headed toward my dorm together at a quicker clip than we had before, I felt myself holding back, offering up less in conversation, deliberately creating more distance between us. When we approached the corner with the entrance to my building, I said goodnight hastily before hurrying inside the glass doors. I couldn't face even the chance that Sam would try to end the night with a kiss. So, just like I did all those times out front of our building in Chinatown the year before, I left him standing alone outside of my dorm as I rushed away. But this time, I didn't look back through the glass.

Once I was back safely inside my room, I hung my coat on a hook behind the bedroom door. I exhaled into the silence as I kicked off my shoes.

———————

I SAT DOWN AT THE SMALL ROUND TABLE IN my dorm room and swept away a few errant crumbs with my fingers before setting my heavy laptop down in front of me. It was 2004, the spring semester of my junior year, and I was studying abroad in London. My grand plans of a Romance Language major had since given way to one in Politics, requiring study in London as opposed to any-where else if I wanted to complete my coursework in time.

In no way was I settling on London—I loved the city and its mélange of historical aspects and modern updates, and I had been placed in a dorm smack in the center of downtown that was filled with other students on the same NYU study abroad program. Walking to and from class each day, I felt the pulse of a city that in many respects wasn't too far of a cry from New York, but at the same time had a different air about it entirely.

I turned and looked over at my two roommates sitting cross-legged on a twin bed talking quietly on the other side of the room, then rolled my eyes and cracked open the computer. The only part of being in London I wasn't par-ticularly enthusiastic about was my rooming situation—while most of the units in my building had one or two occupants each, I had been assigned to a unique, slightly larger room with two others, and three felt like too many to have in one space with no walls between us.

During an orientation event in a large auditorium on the first day of the program, I had spotted a familiar face that made me stop talking mid-sentence. I immediately recognized the light brown hair, the hazel eyes, the distinctive nose, the handsome features. He was standing up several rows ahead of me, looking back as the crowd filed in. *Ben.* I felt my stomach sink as I reflexively looked away. Besides a handful of grocery store sightings from a distance in New York, I had not seen much of him since he had let me down ever-so-gently in the hallway outside his dorm suite last year after our one perfect date. *Ugh. HE, of all people, is in London?*

Later that day, much to my chagrin, I noticed that Ben had been placed in the same dorm as me. The study abroad program was small compared to the spread out, often impersonal nature of the general way of things at NYU, and I had already begun to lament the loss of my anonymity. I really didn't want to have to see someone daily who had broken my heart, though, and in my home of all places.

A little while later on the first day, after my two roommates had left our room, I had just finished unpacking and settling in and was getting ready to head out to find something to do. Our door, the first on the left when you entered our floor, was still propped open as it had been when we first arrived. I walked out of our ensuite bathroom, about to grab my purse, when I suddenly found myself face-to-face with Ben.

"Oh—hey!" I said, startled and confused to see him standing awkwardly in the center of the room, looking almost unsure as to why he had come. *WHAT are you doing here?*

As I got ready to ask if he was looking for someone else, he finally spoke.

"Hey."

His eyes were earnest, and he was standing only a few feet from me as he spoke. It felt oddly close, but I also wasn't sure whether or not I should move.

He continued, "I just wanted to come by and say I'm sorry for everything that happened last year."

I stared at him, trying to make sense of the words. I had written him off in my mind, scratched him from my life. Why was he now standing in front of me saying this? It didn't compute.

"Oh, OK, thanks," I said coolly. "It's OK. I appreciate you coming by."

Ben didn't move. *Anything else?* It seemed like there was more he wanted to say as he lingered there, but he just stood looking at me silently. I glanced uncomfortably at the door and then back at him.

As though snapping out of a trance, he said, "OK, well, I guess I'll be seeing you around."

I nodded, "Yep, see you around."

I was alone again, standing in the center of the room trying to reflect on what had just happened. *What the hell was that?* I understood if Ben wanted to try and be on better terms since we were going to be spending the next several months seeing each other everywhere. But why was he so awkward about it? He was the one who had hurt me when it was obvious that I had liked him; he had the upper hand here. And why did he linger like that? Did he actually have feelings for me? *No.* I refused to allow myself to even go there in my mind. I sighed deeply, picked up my bag, and closed the door behind me as I left the room.

That night, when my relationship with my new roommates was green and still held promise, I had explained to them my short history with Ben. Only a few days later, I learned that one of them liked him, very much as a friend, and possibly also romantically, which unbeknownst to me at the time essentially spelled out the beginning of the end of any kind of real friendship with her. She and our third roommate had since that time become joined at the hip, while I was left out on my own, but the arrangement was mutual.

Now, several weeks into our trip, I sat down at the round table in our room with my laptop in an effort to mentally escape. It was pouring outside, so my now ordinary habit of wandering the busy, historic London streets on my own wasn't much of an option at the moment. I popped in a CD I had brought to access AOL and wondered which friends of mine might be online. I exhaled when I was finally signed in, grateful to see the familiar digital backdrop. I quickly scanned over my Buddy List, and my eyes stopped on a name—Gr8tefulDd1023. I hadn't talked to Jared in months. Our friendship had begun to wane our sophomore year after it had started to sufficiently bother me that we still had a weirdly close connection while he was in a real relationship with someone else.

It had been so long since we had talked, though, that I didn't feel any resentment. I was in the mood to talk to a good friend, someone that knew me, and I thought he might appreciate knowing where I was sitting at the moment. So I double-clicked on his name.

> **JeSslcA148:** Hi from London!

He responded immediately.

> **Gr8tefulDd1023:** Hi from Nicaragua!
> **JeSslcA148:** Wow! Study abroad?
> **Gr8tefulDd1023:** Yep =) You too?
> **JeSslcA148:** Indeed
> **JeSslcA148:** So how's it going?
> **Gr8tefulDd1023:** It's really fantastic.
> **Gr8tefulDd1023:** I feel like I've really been able to immerse myself in the people and culture here.
> **JeSslcA148:** That's awesome
> **Gr8tefulDd1023:** I actually took a page from your book...
> **Gr8tefulDd1023:** Decided before the trip that I wanted to take it all in and make the most of the experience, so I could really remember it when I came back

I felt a light tug on my heartstrings. *He remembered what I had said about Israel.* I was touched that he recalled my words from one of our many late night conversations freshman year. The memory felt bittersweet, though, since so much had changed since then and we had drifted apart since that time. On the one hand, it felt significant that we were connecting online from two such distinctly different places: me in the heart of London and him in some unspecified part of Nicaragua. But I hadn't even known he was going there, and he didn't know my study abroad plans. We weren't really in each other's lives anymore. My initial optimism talking to Jared quickly gave way to a pang of sadness as I realized that despite our across-the-world connection, I now felt more disconnected from him than ever.

"DID YOU DO USY?" ALICIA ASKED ME AS SHE sat down cross-legged on her narrow twin bed, her light brown curly ponytail bouncing as she talked.

It was senior year now, and Alicia was my new roommate. We had met through mutual friends last fall and hit it off before we both went on our respective trips abroad then decided to room together for our last year.

"Um, YES," I said emphatically as I unloaded a few books from my black backpack onto my desk. I turned to face her now. "Very much so. Like, all the conventions, international conventions, Israel Pilgrimage. You did too?"

Alicia nodded. "I was in METNY," she said, naming the region that I knew encompassed parts of New Jersey and New York City.

I felt my heart flutter slightly. "I knew someone from METNY. Did you know Jared Glazer?"

The question flew out of my mouth almost involuntarily. Jared and I were barely in touch anymore but hearing someone mention his region of our youth group called him to mind in spite of myself.

I watched Alicia's eyes widen as her eyebrows shot up. "Wait, how do you know Jared Glazer?"

I sat down on my twin bed now on the wall opposite of hers, about a yard and a half away. I folded my legs under me, matching her cross-legged position, and smiled broadly. "How do YOU know Jared Glazer?"

"We dated for a little bit," she said, and then added succinctly, "He's cheap."

It was clear from the disgusted look on Alicia's face that this was the reason it did not work out between them. I gave a small laugh, unsure what to make of her comment.

"But wait, what about you?" she asked me now.

I paused for a moment, trying to figure out exactly how to describe what Jared and I were, then or now.

"We almost sort of dated also," I finally said.

Alicia shook her head, her light blue eyes twinkling. "Too funny!" She then jumped up and sat down at her desk, having already mentally moved on to something else.

I continued sitting where I was on my bed, ruminating. I hadn't even so much as thought about Jared in a long time now. I replayed in my mind what Alicia had just said: "He's cheap." I tried to hide a smile as I remembered the one meal we had eaten out in New York on my important visit just after freshman year, on our first real date of sorts. I pictured the greasy street cart breadstick in its red and white checkered wax paper that I had consumed with resignation.

Subpar dinner choice notwithstanding, it felt nice to have Jared come up in conversation, and it seemed significant, maybe, that I had found a mutual connection between us. Maybe it was a sign that it was time to reach out.

I walked around to my small wooden desk that backed up to Alicia's desk chair with about five inches between us and moved the trackpad on my laptop. I looked at my Buddy List. Gr8tefulDd1023. He was online. I double clicked on his name to open a message window.

> **JeSslcA148:** Hey!
> **Gr8tefulDd1023:** Hey there!

He was always so quick to respond, it seemed, no matter what our life circumstances were nor how much time had passed.

> **JeSslcA148:** I hear you know Alicia Abramson
> **Gr8tefulDd1023:** This is true. How do you know Alicia Abramson?
> **JeSslcA148:** She's my roommate! And my friend, we chose to live together.
> **Gr8tefulDd1023:** Aha, I didn't know she ended up at NYU. Tell her hi.

JeSslcA148: I will! She's right behind me.
Gr8tefulDd1023: Small world.
Gr8tefulDd1023: I guess I can't be surprised that you guys get along.
Gr8tefulDd1023: You're both the one that got away =)

———————

THE EXPANSIVE, AIRY, MULTI-LEVEL CONVEN-tion space was overflowing with Jewish college students. It was December of my senior year, and I was in Jerusalem, Israel on a political-oriented leadership trip. Each day of the program was jam-packed with speakers, events, and activities, all spent with the limited group I was traveling with from colleges around the country. Tonight, though, we were at a large-scale event that brought together students from all over the United States who were traveling through Israel at the same time. There was no agenda for the evening; they had simply thrown together thousands of young American Jews in what was meant to be a massive opportunity to network and socialize.

Feeling slightly overwhelmed, I wandered the space on my own, stopping to look at some of the keychains, pens, and other swag laid out on vendor tables. I mindlessly stepped onto an escalator, and as it carried me up to the next level, I gazed down at the hordes of faces milling about amidst the buzz of many simultaneous conversations. I looked back up, feeling a bit weary from the limited amount of sleep I was running on, given the late nights and early mornings required of my program. *I hope we don't have to stay here long.*

I walked along the upper level for a moment then decided I would find the escalator to take me back down from the other side. As I walked in that direction, a group of several people was approaching from the other way. I paused when a face among them caught my eye—a guy that looked familiar. I saw brown stubble on his face, and short, dark brown hair spiked up in the front. I realized then why he had captured my attention. *He looks like Avi.*

I had barely thought about Avi since the last day of camp two and a half years before when we parted ways after the group photo at the Camp Laurelwood sign. I thought for a moment about how I was in Israel, his home country. *Maybe that's why that guy reminds me of him.* I realized that the trip had been so busy that I hadn't even stopped to wonder about my Israeli friends from camp and what they might be up to. I lamented that I hadn't even thought to reach out to them to let them know that I was going to be here. Not that I had any free time, anyway.

The group was now just about to pass me. As they did, I glanced over again at the guy who looked like Avi. At that very moment, his face broke out into a huge smile in response to something someone said to him, his grin radiating brighter than the light bulbs on the high ceiling way above us as his dark eyes shone with a mischievous glimmer. My breath caught in my throat as I stared at him, stunned. *Holy shit, it IS Avi.*

"Avi!" I yelled out quickly, before he was out of earshot.

He turned his head in my direction.

"Hey! It's Jessica." I gestured toward myself. "From Camp Laurelwood."

He stopped walking now and looked at me, his eyes momentarily shadowed with a mixture of surprise and confusion. I watched as bewilderment quickly gave way to recognition and familiarity. His intense brown eyes lit up as he studied my face, his brow slightly furrowed.

"Wow, hey! What are you doing here?"

I gestured down at the sea of heads below. "I'm on a school trip here, like everyone else. It's a political action trip."

I thought of all the things I would love to tell him about my trip, how interesting it would be to have his Israeli perspective on it all. I realized then that he wasn't an American college student, though, so I gave him a puzzled look and shook my head slightly.

"What are YOU doing here?"

Avi gestured toward the group he was with. "I work for Hillel at the University of Arizona," he explained, referencing the Jewish student group on campus. "I traveled here with the students."

I felt mystified to learn that he wasn't in this room because he lived in Israel but because he had traveled here, just like me.

"Wow, I had no idea you were in the U.S.," I said as I stared at him, still shocked that he was standing in front of me.

Somewhere I still had that photo of the counselors posing around the camp sign, and I never thought I would see his face again aside from in that shot.

Someone called out Avi's name then, and he looked past me for a moment.

"Well I need to run, but we should stay in touch?" He asked hurriedly.

"Yes, definitely!" I said without hesitation.

It was comforting to see a familiar face in an ocean of so many that were unknown.

Avi found a pen and tore a tiny bit of paper from a document that he was carrying. He scrawled down his name and phone number and handed it to me, his dark eyes fixed on me, eyebrows slightly raised.

"It was nice to see you!" he said with a small smile.

Before I could get out much more than a smile and partial nod in return, he was gone, swept away into the crowd. I looked down at the scrap of paper I held in my hand and shook my head again, still in disbelief that I had just seen him. What were the odds, in this room with so many people, in a country where he was from but neither of us lived, that we would directly cross paths, and moreover, that I would spot him? Did it mean something? So much time had passed, and so many things had happened in my life since camp that I no longer held any anger or ill feelings toward Avi. It simply felt nice to see him in such an odd environment. I carefully folded the piece of paper and stuck it deep into my pocket, knowing it was much too precious to lose. *Maybe our story isn't over yet after all.*

I WALKED EASTWARD ON FOURTEENTH STREET toward my dorm, enjoying the sun on my face. It was the spring semester of my senior year, and studying politics had led me to decide that law school was the path for me. I had submitted all of my applications and was now waiting to hear back from each of the schools, the fate of my next three years yet to be decided. The weather was nice in New York for the first time in days, so I walked a bit slower as I approached my building, basking in the warmth. For a moment, as I began to wonder when I would start hearing back from law schools, I thought of the other potential path I had been considering for next year: an immersive trip to Israel. I felt satisfied with my decision to keep moving forward with my education given that I knew what I wanted, rather than taking a break to delay what I felt was inevitable. I knew I would return to Israel someday anyway.

I remembered the last time I was there, on the political action trip several months before. I thought about the tiny slip of paper that I had stuck in my wallet after that trip. *Avi. Were we meant to stay in touch?* It felt like there had to have been a reason why I had run into him that day last December, some greater purpose that led to the two of us crossing paths in that moment.

I decided that I didn't want to wonder. It was sunny outside. I was feeling great. *I'm going to call him.* When I approached my dorm, I stood just outside and pulled my light purple leather wallet out of my bag. I shot a quick look in each direction then discreetly opened up the billfold pocket. Behind a couple twenties I found the bit of paper, tucked in carefully for safekeeping. I gingerly pulled it out, unfolded it, and studied Avi's first and last name scrawled in all capital letters with a phone number underneath, all in black ink. I took a deep breath then pulled out my cell phone and dialed.

As I listened to the line ring on the other end, I realized I didn't really know why I was calling him or what I would say. Before I could change my mind and hang up, I heard someone pick up.

"Hello?" said a slightly-accented voice.

"Hey, is this Avi?" I asked, trying to regulate my breathing so my voice didn't sound nervous. *Be cool.*

"This is," he said back formally.

"It's Jessica . . . from camp? I saw you in Israel a couple months ago?"

There was silence on the line for a moment.

"Oh yeah, hey!" he finally said. "What's going on?"

I sighed. *Why did I call him again?* It was too late now. I took another deep breath, tilting the phone away from my mouth as I exhaled so he couldn't hear it.

"Not much, I'm just on my way back from class. I remembered that I had your number, so I figured I would give you a call."

"Nice, nice, OK . . ."

There was a long pause, and I felt my chest rising and falling quickly.

"Well, I thought it was really cool running into you!" I said, breaking the silence.

"Yeah, yeah, that was amazing!" He said. "It's a small world."

Before I could say anything else, he spoke again. "Well I actually have to run right now. But thanks for calling!"

We said goodbye, and then I heard a *click*.

I stood on the sidewalk outside my dorm feeling embarrassed and a bit dejected as people passed by me in either direction. Two male students with backpacks were walking toward the dorm, and an older man with a white beard wearing large headphones and carrying a slice of pizza on a paper plate was going the other way. I don't know exactly what I had been expecting from the call, beyond my attempt to unearth some meaning from our chance encounter. I wanted him to believe our run-in was significant, maybe even somewhat magical, like I had. But on the phone, it had felt like there was nothing to say to each other, and he didn't even seem to understand why I was calling. Whatever I had been seeking, I most certainly did not find it. I remembered then how Avi had let me down during our summer at camp, and I was not surprised to again find myself disappointed in his wake. *Maybe our story is over. He's just a guy that I liked once.* And maybe it wasn't so miraculous that I had run into him again after all.

CHAPTER NINE

You Should Have Just Thrown a Martini in My Face

AND THEN IT WAS THE END OF 2005. I HAD landed in Washington, DC for law school at American University. The first semester had been a whirlwind of highlighted case law books, daunting professors, and weekends filled with reading at coffee shops during the days and drinking with new friends at night. But now, it was finally winter break. I had come home to Pennsylvania for several days and had just decided to do a short visit to New York to see some friends.

Sitting at the computer in the family room of my parents' house while I was making my plans, I saw that Jared was online, and I felt my breath catch in my chest slightly. Despite occasional IMs while I was in school, we had barely been in touch over the last several years at all. Still, being at home made me think of him. And I was planning a trip to New York, a place that was still somehow synonymous with him in my mind. I looked at his name on my Buddy List: Gr8tefulDd1023. I knew he had moved back to the city after college, and I was pretty sure I had recently noticed on Facebook that he was single now.

I sighed as I remembered chatting with him online from this very computer that summer after our freshman year before everything had gotten so real for me that it had to end. I turned and looked over my shoulder at the beige leather couch, and in my mind I could see us sitting there during his visit, snuggling together and pretending to watch TV. *Is it possible that he was the right person for me but our timing had just been wrong?* It was a thought I had periodically entertained since I started to miss him during our sophomore year. I shook my head quickly. I truly had no idea. *Well there's no harm in saying hi.*

> **JeSslcA148:** Hey Jared
> **Gr8tefulDd1023:** Hey there
> **JeSslcA148:** How's it going? Are you home in NY?
> **Gr8tefulDd1023:** I am indeed! How's about you?
> **JeSslcA148:** I'm home in PA

For a moment I debated whether I should mention I was coming to New York. We had not seen each other since that pivotal summer when I was at camp and we met up on the Fourth of July, now three and a half years before. After that we had mostly gone our separate ways. Did he even want to see me? I took a deep breath and continued typing.

> **JeSslcA148:** I'm headed to NY tomorrow for the weekend
>
> **Gr8tefulDd1023:** Nice! Got any plans?
>
> **JeSslcA148:** Staying with my grandfather and meeting up with some friends
>
> **JeSslcA148:** But I actually have some time on Sunday...are you around?
>
> **Gr8tefulDd1023:** Hmmmm...Sunday
>
> **Gr8tefulDd1023:** Yeah!
>
> **Gr8tefulDd1023:** I've got something to do in the morning, and also later in the day, but I should have some time in the afternoon.
>
> **Gr8tefulDd1023:** That work?
>
> **JeSslcA148:** Yeah! Let's figure it out...
>
> **JeSslcA148:** I have to get a bus back to PA at 3pm that day.

It was fun scheming plans for a New York meet-up with Jared; it was reminiscent of how things were during an earlier time. We chatted for a bit longer and ultimately made plans to meet around noon that Sunday at Penn Station, where he would arrive on a train from Queens. I signed offline, smiling. I was going to see Jared in New York. I had no idea what to expect, but I was excited for the chance to see him nonetheless.

———————

I WALKED TOWARD PENN STATION ROLLING A tiny suitcase behind me. It was such a small piece of luggage that its long handle was comical, but it fit my items for the weekend, and so it accompanied me now. The air was cold, so I was grateful to be wearing a black scarf looped around my neck over my lavender wool coat.

I stopped among a crowd of people at a busy corner and waited for the light to change. As I crossed the street and made my way toward Penn Station, I couldn't help but think back to when I met Jared in New York that first time after our freshman year. I had been so excited when I rode the bus into the city that day, at a moment when the road was open before me and all things represented an adventure I had yet to conquer—that summer at a new camp, a new life at NYU in the fall, and the rosy promise about what could happen between Jared and me.

Now I felt like a different, more grounded version of my wide-eyed, adventurous nineteen-year-old self. I was on a specific career path, and though slightly less of the world was open to me, I liked it this way. I was happy in law school and felt at home in DC. I generally had the sensation that I was on an avenue that was right for me. I had no idea whether or not Jared would be interested in the version of me that I was now, nor did I know whether or not I was interested in him.

I pushed the sleeve of my coat back from my left wrist and glanced at my square-faced watch. 11:55 a.m. Jared's train was slated to arrive at 12:05 p.m. *Just barely enough time to see what I look like.* As I rode the escalator down into Penn Station, I was suddenly nervous in spite of myself. It had been so long since we had seen each other, and we had barely even stayed in touch as friends during that time. Now we were both single, out of college, and living in the world. Maybe things would be different. I followed the signs to the ladies room, then quickly pulled open the stained metal door. *Seriously, how can they have a bathroom this small in a train station?*

I stood in front of one of two tiny metal sinks and washed my hands. Briefly I glanced through the mirror at the woman next to me. Her dandelion-yellow hair was in disarray, and I watched as she brushed her teeth and spit into the sink. I quickly averted my eyes and checked my makeup. I pulled out my lip gloss to glaze on another coat. Then I fluffed my hair, looked at my watch, and exhaled. What was I about to walk into? I stepped back out into the noisy corridor. *Well, here we go.*

By the time I arrived back at the spot where Jared and I had agreed to meet, I could already see him walking in a crowd of people that were headed in my direction. He wore a black leather jacket, and his curly hair and kind eyes looked the same as I remembered.

"Hey!" he said with a broad smile.

We hugged delicately like acquaintances with little emotional association to each other. *Hmm. Maybe there won't be anything this time around.* Jared seemed at once the same and different. I didn't feel anything in particular for him; it felt more like encountering someone I used to have some things in common with rather than a person I had any demonstrable connection with in the present. But we were in New York, and it was December, a time when the city would provide a sparklingly enchanted backdrop no matter what we did. At the very least, we could have a fun time as friends. I silently vowed to make the best of the afternoon.

"So how was your trip in?" I asked.

Jared smiled and shrugged. "Eh, fine. The usual."

As we walked together in the direction of the exit, he turned to look at me. "So, do anything fun this weekend?"

I nodded, rolling my suitcase behind me. "Yeah, it was good to be here and catch up with friends."

I studied his face as I spoke, looking for something, anything, that would give me an indication of whether or not he was still interested in me. I came up with nothing.

I put on a friendly smile. "Well, thanks for meeting up!"

Jared grinned back. "Of course! If you're here, it's easy for me." He stuck both hands into his coat pockets. "So, what should we do?"

I shrugged. "I'm open! It would be nice to just walk around. Maybe a museum?"

We turned a corner into throngs of people waiting to go up an escalator.

"I'm always good for walking," he said. "I think the MoMa is pretty close."

I smiled and nodded. "That's perfect! I've only been to the one in Queens."

We stepped onto the escalator, and I could smell the tantalizing aroma of freshly roasted nuts wafting through the air from a nearby street cart as we were carried up toward the sidewalk. Jared stood on the step just above me, and I enjoyed how close we were as I looked up at him.

He eyed the suitcase propped beside me. "So what's with the luggage?"

I gave a small laugh. "I know, it's annoying. But I'm going straight to the bus later so I had to bring it with me. I wish New York had lockers or something."

Jared shrugged. "Yeah, that would be nice, wouldn't it? Oh well, at least it's pretty small. It shouldn't give you too much trouble on our walk."

I mentally noted that he had not made an offer to help, but I shook my head. "Oh, it's fine, I'm used to it by now! It's been with me all weekend."

As we stepped off the escalator and onto the sidewalk, for a brief moment one wheel of the suitcase caught on the last step before I dislodged it just in time. I sighed as I resettled it onto the flat surface behind me then looked up at the street sign on the corner to orient myself. As Jared led us north on Seventh Avenue, I had to carefully weave around the steady flow of passersby in order to fit through with the bag behind me. I peeked at Jared out of the corner of my eye as we crossed a street. *Still no offer to assist. Friends indeed?*

He looked at me. "If we go all the way up to Fifty-Fourth, we're basically right there. Can you handle the suitcase that far?"

I nodded slowly with a small smile to myself. "Yeah, I got it."

Thankfully, I was reprieved of the suitcase when we arrived at the MoMA and a uniformed security officer pointed to it and required that I leave it up front with him. As Jared and I wandered into the museum together, my mind flashed back to our first meeting in New York when we had meandered around the Museum of Natural History together. So excited to be seeing each other in person for the first time after a year of build-up, we were exponentially more focused on our conversation than the exhibits that surrounded us. So much had changed since then. Now, we walked slowly across the tiled floor on the ground level past a sculpture of giant spheres of various colors and sizes and into a room with walls lined with paintings and drawings. Jared drifted toward the left side of the room, and I diverged to the right, studying a row of paintings that caught my eye.

I stopped in front of a picture that was completely blank except for a small painting of a 1950s gas station in the lower righthand corner with an old fashioned car parked out front. Suddenly I heard a voice behind me, jarring me as it broke through the quiet, contemplative silence of the space.

"Sometimes I just don't get modern art. I try to—I really do—but I feel like if it's something I could have made myself as a child, why is it famous?"

I blinked and turned to look at Jared. I had just been admiring the picture again after reading the description on the small golden plaque next to its frame.

"Oh, I like it," I managed. "I get it though, I used to feel that way about modern art until I studied it for a bit in college, and now I've actually come to appreciate it."

I turned back to continue on to the next painting and noticed that Jared was in lockstep by my side. I felt slightly annoyed. *Is this how the whole museum visit is going to go?*

About thirty minutes later we were back on the street. Despite its awkward beginning, the rest of our time at the museum had mostly involved us wandering into rooms together but studying the art separately. By the time we were next to each other again outside, I felt rejuvenated and again hopeful about the day. I was in New York with Jared, and that felt meaningful in its own right. A moderate wind was blowing now, making the air feel even colder than it was before. I pulled a pair of black leather gloves from my pockets and slipped them on.

"Aren't we right near all the Christmas decorations?" I asked.

"Oh yeah," he said with a broad smile. "The big tree is right around the corner."

We walked together in that direction and my eyes lit up as we rounded the corner to face a gigantic Christmas tree covered in tiny white lights towering over us. Cheerful holiday music was playing around us, and people were milling in all directions. I stopped to take in the scene. *Now this is romantic no matter what Jared and I are.* We made our way through the crowd until we were just in front of the tree. I gazed up at its soaring branches then looked at Jared next to me, his face turned upward. It felt like the first time I had gotten a proper opportunity to take a good long look at him. He was attractive in his black leather coat and jeans with soft gray gloves on his hands and a gray knit scarf slung around his neck. I wondered what he was thinking about, then I looked back up at the tree.

"I haven't seen this since I was a kid. Not even during all the time that I was in the city for school."

Jared smiled. "I mean, you gotta see the tree."

Taken by the romanticism of the moment, I realized that I was going to want to remember it. Who knew, maybe one day I would look back on this as the tentative start of something. Maybe now it was the right time for us.

"Hey, can we ask someone to take our picture?" I asked as I pulled a tiny silver digital camera out from the front pocket of my suitcase. I tapped the shoulder of a middle-aged blonde woman in a red hat as she passed us.

After handing her my camera, I walked back in front of the tree and Jared slid his left arm around my back. I wrapped my right arm around his shoulders, and as the picture was snapped, I felt a warm sense of comfort. Jared, me, and my suitcase, captured for posterity.

Jared glanced at his watch. "What time did you need to catch the bus?"

I looked at my own wrist. "I need to be at the bus station in about an hour.

Jared nodded. "Let's head in that direction then."

As we trekked toward the station, we passed a street vendor selling large plastic glasses covered in silver glitter that spelled out "2006" with cutouts for the eyes where the two zeros were. I stopped and reached out to touch a pair, running my fingers over the glitter.

"I find these completely hilarious for some reason. Hang on, I'm going to get a pair."

I still wanted to remember this day with Jared, even though I wasn't sure why. I handed a five dollar bill to the man in a black beanie who was slouched in his folding chair next to the display.

"Merry Christmas," he said with a nod.

I smiled, put the glasses on, and looked at Jared. "What do you think?"

His eyes sparkled as he chuckled. "They're totally you."

I pushed them up onto the top of my head where they stayed for the rest of the walk.

When I saw that we were approaching the block with the bus station, I checked the time again. It was just before 2 p.m.

"I have a little bit of time, so I'm probably going to grab some food," I told Jared. "Do you want to come?"

He nodded. "Yeah, sure, I've got some time also."

Perfect, I thought, remembering some of the quaint and romantic-looking restaurants we had passed a block or two back. *Maybe this will finally be our moment.*

Jared looked up the block and gestured toward the Subway sandwich shop just ahead of us. "How 'bout here?"

My heart sank slightly, but I shrugged my shoulders. "Sure, works for me."

As I stood in line looking up at the neon-backlit menu board inset with pictures of sub sandwiches, I watched Jared step up to the counter to place his order. In my mind I saw my senior year roommate Alicia, just after she and I had discovered that we had Jared in common. "He's cheap," she had said so matter-of-factly. I hid a small smile with my hand as I moved forward to take my turn at the counter.

After some unremarkable moments spent stuffing our faces with giant subs, we were soon back on the street walking toward the bus station. There was a strong wind now and it had gotten significantly colder outside, so I ducked my head down slightly as we walked. Soon we stopped and faced each other in front of the station. Jared looked up at the festive glasses still perched on top of my head.

"Those are totally leaving glitter in your hair," he said as he pulled off the gray glove from his right hand. He reached up and gingerly brushed away some shiny silver flecks from my hair with his finger before gently blowing them into the air.

I smiled and felt my face flush slightly from his touch.

"Are you good from here?" he asked. "Unfortunately I have to run to meet up with my buddy. Today is his last day in town, and I promised I'd catch him before he leaves."

I nodded. "My suitcase and I? We're like THIS now." I held up my right hand with middle and index fingers crossed. "Yeah, I'm good. Thanks for hanging out."

Jared nodded. "OK then. Safe travels home."

We hugged, our embrace longer and warmer than the cursory one we had shared at Penn Station earlier in the day. I felt the soft wool of his gray scarf beneath my chin as my arms clasped around his back.

A little while later, I sat on the bus looking out the window as I waited for the driver to pull out of the station. I sighed and remembered back to three and a half years before when I had sat on a bus at the exact same gate and Jared had kissed me gently before saying goodbye. So much had changed since then. Today, he hadn't even walked into the station with me. We were friends, and I wasn't even sure how close anymore. I pulled the plastic glasses off my head and folded them in my lap. *2006.* They sparkled with such promise, reflecting back the tiny round lights above my seat. I had hoped that seeing Jared would elicit some sort of clarity in my mind about how I felt about him or that I would gain a sense of where he was coming from or where we stood. A part of me had hoped that the magic of the city might somehow recreate the emotions we felt for each other in the past. I wanted him to look at me the way he looked at me back then, so I could get my second chance. But he didn't, and I didn't, and now I sat on the bus to leave the city in exactly the same place as when I had arrived. I leaned back deeper into my seat, settling in for the ride. As the bus slowly turned out onto the busy street, I gazed out the window again. *Maybe I'll never know whether we were supposed to be something but missed our opportunity.*

———

I SAT BACK DOWN IN THE BLACK DESK CHAIR at the front of the law school admissions office after finishing a tour of the school to a prospective student. During my first summer of law school, I had picked up a few part time jobs, one of which was working at the school admissions desk. It worked out nicely; when I wasn't answering phones or giving a tour, I was able to sit at the front desk computer and edit a document I was working on for a professor, or else I could just play on my email or chat with friends.

The office seemed quiet now, so I clicked open my Gmail account. I glanced at a recent email thread from Jared. We had kept in better touch after seeing each other in New York, and I had learned soon after that he was looking for jobs in DC. We had always had some overlapping interests in government and policy, so it did not surprise me that he was interested in moving here. Very recently we had been emailing back and forth a lot, since he had found a job here and was working on relocating.

We had also been instant messaging each other often; I had recently adopted Google Talk, or "Gchat," over AIM as my primary chat medium once I realized that it was more discreet to use during class and that most of my friends had started to switch over anyway. Now that Jared and I were chat buddies again, we found ourselves in touch more regularly than we had been since our early college days. Just as I was looking at our email thread, wondering whether or not he had moved into his new apartment yet, I saw a chat message pop up.

> **Jared:** Hey!
> **Jared:** I'm here. :)
> **Jared:** Just finished moving into my place.

Jared: Got everything but a table

Jared: Which I'll need if you're going to join me at it anytime soon :)

me: Hey! That's awesome!

me: Welcome!

me: Well we'll have to get together

Jared: Yes, definitely!

Jared: Possibly later on today. If not, then tomorrow.

I felt a familiar flutter in my stomach at the thought of seeing Jared so soon. I had continued to hold in the back of my mind the possibility that now that I had grown up a bit, there might be a bona fide chance for us. And now, he was here in DC—for the first time ever in all the time that I had known him, we would be living in the same place. Maybe, maybe, it was finally our time. Or at the very least, our time to try.

I had recently broken up with my first real boyfriend, who I had met in law school during the spring semester of my first year and dated for a few months. Jared knew about the breakup since we had been messaging each other on a regular basis recently. Confiding in him, I secretly hoped that because he knew I was single, and because our conversations had angled toward being slightly more intimate as of late, that this could be the beginning of us getting close again, this time at the right time.

I couldn't hold back a giant smile as I continued typing. *He's here.*

me: No problem. I'm sure you have tons of
settling in to do
me: Let me know when works for you and I'd
love to meet up
Jared: Definitely.
Jared: Today I'm guessing I'll be with
Samantha for most of the day. She lives in
DC, we met when I was still in NY
Jared: We've been doing the long distance
thing, but we recently became official now
that I've moved here :)

My cheeks went cold as the smile quickly evaporated
from my face. I had thought that at last, our timing had
aligned. Familiar feelings of confusion and disappointment
washed over me. I was transported back to our sophomore
year of college, after I had ended things with Jared but
knew I missed him and wanted to stay in touch, but he was
already taken. I remembered how uncomfortable it made
me feel that we still had what felt like a close relationship in
spite of the fact that he was with someone else.

So long ago, we had been in a boat together, sailing
along with the world open in front of us. After I bailed
and swam away, he had immediately pulled the next girl
into the boat with him. Even after I later realized I might
have swam away too quickly, I had never made it back into
the boat again. Instead, I floated nearby on a paddle board
with an oar in my hands, trying my darnedest to stay near
his boat while also trying to stay afloat so I could make sure

I was there when the moment was finally right for us to ride off again together.

A crackling anger seeped into my veins, drowning out the disappointment, and I knew all at once that I was in no way willing to go through what I went through before. I wouldn't be that girl anymore that Jared talked to on the side who was always left wondering, worried that she had missed her chance, frantically paddling near his boat and hoping for another shot. *I can't do this anymore.*

With this newly gleaned information on his relationship status, I was bothered by the way Jared had been connecting with me recently—still flirtatious, still acting like a confidante. Maybe I had grown up more. I was happy in DC, I had friends here, I was on a career path, and the last thing I wanted was to feel any more of those confused emotions that I had felt toward him during my sophomore year. I was past all of that. The prospect of going backward in time, of finding myself again chasing after a Jared that had long since moved on, was no longer an option for me. My jaw fixed, I stared straight ahead at the computer and began typing back.

> **me:** Oh, wow, I didn't know you were dating someone.
> **me:** I'm sorry to say this, but I think it's probably for the best if we actually go our separate ways.
> **me:** Good luck with settling into DC.
> **Jared:** ....

Jared: Wait, what?

Jared: I thought we were friends...

I felt a tug of my heartstrings. Ever since I had ended things with him before they had even formally started so long ago, we had never been anything other than friends. But I knew I couldn't be there for him, not now, not given our history, not given my conflicting emotions, nor his mixed signals. Before I could change my mind, I promptly blocked him from my chat list so he could no longer message me.

I put my head into my hands and leaned on the desk in front of me, sighing deeply. I felt exhausted and deflated from having gone from eminently hopeful to exceedingly distressed in such a short span of time. I knew I had made the right decision.

———

"THIS WORKS OUT WELL BECAUSE AFTER THE way today has gone, I could *really* use a martini," Jackie was saying as we walked up to the entrance doors of the Adas Israel Synagogue in Northwest DC.

Jackie was a friend from USY back in high school, and we had recently reconnected when she moved to Northern Virginia just outside DC. It was a Thursday night in 2006, deep into the fall semester of my second year of law school.

I laughed at Jackie's comment. "Yeah, I'm guessing they'll have a martini or two. Or three."

Jackie chuckled as we walked through the glass doors on the side of the synagogue. "It is called the 'Three Martinis Celebration,' so there better be!"

The name of the event, a young professionals gathering celebrating the Jewish holiday of Simchat Torah, had caught our eye, and so here we were.

We walked into a long, rectangular room with broad windows on the left wall letting some of the remaining October daylight stream onto the shiny wooden floor. Immediately to our right was a small square table draped with a white tablecloth and lined with rows and rows of neon blue, green, and pink martinis rising up on a tiered display. There were only a handful of other people in the room so far, so in an effort to stave off any awkwardness, Jackie and I quickly reached for martinis. I snatched up a green one, and she grabbed a pink.

I glanced down at the neon green drink practically glowing in my hand, then shrugged and brought the large glass to my lips to take a sip. I let only a very small amount of liquid into my mouth, but I still winced at the potency of the alcohol and the strong, sour flavor. I knew that the drink would act more as a prop than an active beverage for the rest of the night. Jackie and I found a place in front of the windows to stand with our drinks, and our eyes drifted toward the entrance when we saw someone else walk in.

I audibly gasped as I inadvertently looked directly into those familiar gray-blue eyes. I took in the unmistakable strong build and the short, sandy, curly hair. *Jared.* Jackie looked over her bright pink martini at me with raised eyebrows. As soon as I recognized him, I instinctively looked away, and I held my gaze in front of me now as I spoke to Jackie.

"I know that guy . . ." I mumbled.

I looked back up and felt my breath catch in my throat when I suddenly saw Jared standing right in front of me; he had clearly beelined directly toward me upon entering the room.

As I looked at him, I noticed that he hadn't even bothered to stop and pick up a martini first. Instead, in his hand he held a thick, well-worn paperback book. *Same as ever. Always with a book, just in case.* In the past, I had admired that and marveled at how cosmopolitan it was. But now, showing up at a young professionals event holding a book just appeared staged to me, as though he was trying too hard to cultivate an intellectual persona. In an instant, and for the first time, I felt like I saw through him.

I finally met Jared's eyes as they looked directly into mine. He had stepped close to me with his shoulders squared toward me in a confrontational stance; looking away was not an option.

Without even acknowledging Jackie's presence, he simply regarded me for a moment, then spoke. "I can't believe you ditched me right when I moved to DC. I didn't know that many people, and you just decided not to talk to me anymore. You were supposed to be my friend." He nearly spit out the last sentence.

I stared back at him as he spoke, my face paralyzed in shock both at the fact that he was standing in front of me and also at the words that he was saying. Unable to formulate a response and unsure where to look, I glanced down and focused in on his book again. I studied the worn spine and noticed the creases that had formed on the front cover from frequent use. The book seemed out of place, as though it was unsure how it had found its way into a room of twenty-something Jewish people mingling with brightly-colored martinis when all it longed for was a quiet, quotidian metro ride. I almost felt sorry for it.

In that instant, Jared turned on his heels and made a straight dash back toward the door from which he had just entered, book still in hand. As I watched him breeze by the martini table, I thought with humor how I was lucky that I got away without getting a neon martini tossed in my face, given how angrily he had just spoken to me before storming off. Getting a drink poured on me would have been a perfect capstone to such an odd moment, but it was merely words he spewed at me so acrimoniously, and my face was dry as Jackie and I watched him disappear through the doorway.

Jackie's voice suddenly jolted me out of my thoughts. "OK, WHAT was that? That guy was PMS-ing or something . . ."

I shook my head. "It's a long story." I absentmindedly raised my drink to my lips and took another sip, immediately regretting it as the pungent flavor filled my mouth again, and I reluctantly gulped it down. I looked back at the door apprehensively, concerned that Jared could reappear again at any moment just as quickly as he had left.

"We kind of dated at one point then stayed in touch," I finally explained. "But when he moved here he was in a relationship, and I still felt like he was flirting with me, so I broke off our friendship," I went on. "I'm guessing that's what that was about. But," I continued, "I don't think THAT was exactly warranted. Did he really just leave?"

Jackie looked at the door, covering a smile with her hand as she nodded slowly. "Dude, that was so awkward. I'm getting another martini—want one?" She glanced down at my still-full glass. "Nah, you're good. Be back."

As I watched her traipse back toward the martini display, I tried to process what had just happened. I felt anger slowly starting to rise inside me as I replayed the scene in my mind. *What right does he have to be so mad at me? He was the one with the girlfriend. And where was she, anyway? And why did he care so much?* I exhaled deeply, and my anger started to soften into a mixture of embarrassment for Jared for his irrational behavior, plus a tinge of guilt for having stopped talking to him and having been unable to be his friend. This was because I knew that it was me who had decided, in the beginning when we were nineteen and had just started to become something, that we couldn't be anything. I watched Jackie set her empty martini glass down on the table and study the lineup of drinks before ultimately picking up a blue one.

The room had started to fill up more, and I was surrounded now by the light hum of upbeat conversation. I felt relieved that the moment with Jared had ended just as suddenly as it had begun, and that he was no longer standing in front of me. I silently hoped that it would be a long time before our paths would cross again, then I thought with some optimism that if we did run into each other any time soon, at least at that point he may be too embarrassed to approach me. *How did we get here?*

––––––––––

LATER THAT FALL, I WAS OUT WITH JACKIE again, this time on a Friday night. We were back at the Adas Israel synagogue for Shabbat services and dinner. We walked into a small sanctuary where the service was to be held and now eyed the rows of seats, seeing that many had already been filled up. I noticed a few open spots at the end of a row near the front and gestured toward them, and we made our way in that direction.

As we settled into our cushioned seats, I reflexively began to scan the room of post-work, young Jewish professionals chatting amongst each other to see if there was anyone I knew. As I looked around, my eyes came to a quick halt and I felt my stomach drop. I only saw the back of his head several rows ahead of me and to the right, but I recognized the close-cropped, light-colored curls immediately. I watched as he turned toward the brunette woman that sat beside him, and his profile was revealed, instantly confirming my suspicions. I sighed deeply. *Jared.* I saw him leaning in closely to the woman next to him as they talked. *And his girlfriend. My lucky day.* I averted my eyes down to the black leather handbag in my lap, then turned slightly toward Jackie and spoke in a low voice.

"That guy . . . remember the one who told me off at the martini thing? He's here."

Jackie turned toward me with wide eyes and a huge grin. "Ooooh . . . better hide, or he'll come yell at you again."

I sighed again and glanced around the room once more. I saw that it was completely full now, so I calculated that I could, conceivably, carefully avoid Jared at the dinner that was to follow and maybe even still have a good time. The night didn't have to be a wash. Plus, I wanted to stay. Events like this were always a great opportunity to meet other Jews in town, and I was single. Knowing Jared was there and might see me and potentially watch anything that I did put a slight damper on the evening, but I decided I wouldn't let it ruin the night entirely.

After the service ended, we were directed to a large ballroom filled with white tablecloth-covered round tables. Jackie and I chose an empty one toward the back of the room and selected seats facing inward so we could still see what was going on. As I gazed out at the sea of tables, well aware that Jared was likely filing into the room just behind me, for the quickest, most fleeting moment my mind flashed back to the night I met him so many years ago in Israel, after a Shabbat dinner, across a room of white tablecloths, that felt like a lifetime ago now. I blinked, remembering how much had happened since then, and how everything had changed.

There were still ample empty tables throughout the vast room, so I was not worried about ending up too close to him.

Plus, I had already chosen a seat, and there was no way he would choose to be anywhere near me. As I talked to Jackie, I kept a lookout for Jared out of the corner of my eye so that I could safely confirm that he had ended up on the opposite side of the room. Once that happened, I planned to forge ahead with my evening as though he was not even here. And then in an instant, Jared appeared, standing over us across the table. The brunette woman he had been sitting next to at the service stood beside him, scowling slightly.

"Are these seats taken?" Jared asked innocently.

Shocked and confused, I shook my head. "Nope, go ahead." *OK, so this is how he's going to play it. Acting like nothing ever happened between us. Fine. I can be mature, too.*

"This is Samantha," Jared said, gesturing to the girl beside him.

I introduced him to Jackie, then as more people streamed into the room, the seats between us quickly began to fill in.

As dinner went on, I kept half expecting there to be some sort of scene between Jared and me, but that moment never came. Jackie and I ended up with interesting people on either side of us that we were able to talk to for the entirety of the meal, so we did not have to engage with Jared and his girlfriend on the opposite side of the table much at all. I was still surprised that he seemed to have gone out of his way to sit with us and introduce me to his girlfriend. However, I was determined to be comparably mature, at least on the surface, and to not let him know how much I was silently seething, or how uncomfortable I felt. *Maybe this is his way of getting back at me for everything. Or maybe he IS actually trying to be mature.* I had not a clue. As soon as the meal was over, I made a quick escape and was soon walking on the sidewalk toward home in the cool night air.

Once back in my apartment, I sat down at my white Ikea desk with a steaming mug of vanilla mint tea in my hands as I reflected on what had just happened. I realized that in spite of myself I actually felt good; I was relieved. I had just seen Jared, with his girlfriend, and we had both acted maturely. Despite how the situation had initially made me feel, no outward emotions were expressed by either of us; there was no confrontation. We had simply existed in the same place, in close proximity, without incident. Maybe things would be OK with us after all; perhaps Jared and I could coexist in the same city without our peculiar history producing any further turmoil.

I took a sip of my tea, savoring the fresh and earthy aroma and the soothing warmth of the liquid on my tongue. As I set the mug back down on the desk in front of me, I felt surprised as I realized that seeing Jared with his girlfriend had not made me feel jealous or sad, nor had it given me the sense that I should be with him instead of her. I took another sip, feeling oddly Zen about the whole situation. Maybe I would never see Jared again, and that would be OK. We had ended on a polite note. Maybe our paths wouldn't cross in the vast ocean of the world anymore, and we could truly break away from each other, once and for all, onward into our respective futures. We would still be part of the same body of water, but the ripples from each of our oars in the deep blue would no longer affect one another. I pulled my chair in closer to my desk and rested my head on my hand, exhaling. *Maybe we are actually growing up.*

———————

I FLOPPED ONTO THE PINK FLOWERED COM-forter of my childhood bed. I lay on my stomach with my legs outstretched behind me, my feet up by the pillow and my head near the foot of the bed. I shifted around to make myself comfortable then reached down with my right hand and pulled my laptop up onto the bed in front of me. Once I had cracked it open and pulled up my Gmail, I opened up Gchat to see which of my friends were online.

It was 2008 now, and I was home for a few days during the winter holiday season. I had graduated law school the prior spring and was working in DC. By this time, I had long since gotten past the point of someone I liked actually liking me back, and I had allowed several real relationships to materialize. I had started dating someone this past summer, a guy that I had met at a Jewish event and discovered was in medical school with my brother Mike. After a whirlwind six months that had moved very quickly and intensely, we had recently broken up, and I had come to visit my parents in Pennsylvania for a change of scenery.

As I scanned the list of my friends online, my eyes stopped on the name Sam Isaacs. After our sole date at the beginning of my junior year at NYU, when I had been unable to join him in the bakery for a bear claw that night in the East Village, we had stayed in loose touch as friends. We became friends on Facebook toward the end of college, and periodically connected when I was in law school, often enough that our friendship eventually migrated over to Gchat as well. I never knew exactly why I couldn't keep enjoying myself with him that night on our date, and I knew I probably would never fully understand. But I liked him as a person and had enjoyed staying in touch in recent years.

We didn't talk very often these days, but when we did, it was usually when we were both home around a holiday, each alone in our quiet hometowns and looking for something to do, or rather, for someone to connect with. I clicked his name now and started to type.

> **me:** Hey, how's it going?
>
> **Sam:** Hey there!
>
> **Sam:** Not bad, chilling at home in Boston. Kinda bored but it's also kinda nice
>
> **me:** I know what you mean!
>
> **me:** It's nice to be away, but it's always nice to get back
>
> **me:** I'm actually really enjoying the refuge of home at the moment, just broke up with someone and it did not end well :-/
>
> **Sam:** Ah, I'm sorry
>
> **Sam:** I know the feeling though...I've sort of been going through a breakup for the last 4 months.

Sam: Slowly peeling off the band aid kind of thing
me: I'm sorry, that sounds tough
Sam: Yeah...I suppose I'm doing it to myself though

A few minutes passed. I wasn't sure what to type back to him. We had gotten real pretty quickly, and I didn't know where to go from here. Luckily, Sam took the conversation in a different direction.

Sam: You're in DC these days?
me: Yep! I love it. Still NY right?
Sam: Brooklyn indeed
me: Still playing music I hope?
Sam: Of course
Sam: I mean I've still got the 9 to 5 for now, but I play whenever I can
Sam: My band has been recording an album actually, with a record label
me: That's awesome! I would love to hear the music sometime
Sam: I'll send you some
Sam: Did you finish law school?
me: I did! Working for the city government in DC now.
Sam: Nice. I've looked at some federal government jobs.

Sam: I told you my brother's been an attorney
for a few years, right?
me: Yeah, he does some kind of finance stuff,
right?
Sam: Yeah. He likes the law life
Sam: So here are some links to our songs...

I sat up cross-legged on my bed now, anxious to hear his music. I thought back to sophomore year, when I had run into him on my way to do laundry, how I had stopped to listen, transfixed. I sighed as I remembered how his soft voice and beautiful guitar strumming had instantly transported me to a place far beyond the walls of our dorm building, to a land completely removed from the bustling city outside of them. It was no surprise to me that he was recording an album now; he was that good.

Excitedly, I clicked on the play button for the first song that he had sent. Expecting to hear soft guitar strumming, I was surprised by the pop-y, computer-generated, electronic beats that emanated from my laptop speakers. *Sounds like The Postal Service.* Then I heard Sam singing over the music. I was immediately soothed by the sound of his voice, but I was caught off guard by how different the overall style was from what I remembered. His simple strumming and gentle singing on the otherwise cold floor of our Chinatown dorm building had been so perfectly simple, so beautifully pure.

I wanted to be excited for him, but I felt strangely disappointed. The genuine restraint of his music felt drowned out by artificial sound, which in my mind diluted and masked his talent. I continued listening to the song, searching. It was energetic and catchy, but nowhere did I find the authenticity I had heard resonating in our dorm hallway so long ago. This song instead felt produced specifically to appeal to a mass audience. Listening to it just made me long for the unadulterated version of Sam and his guitar that I had known before, the pale boy in the faded jean jacket with brightly colored patches who had contemplatively smoked cigarettes outside our NYU building. It felt like he had sold out.

> **me:** It's catchy. It's good
>
> **me:** To be honest though, I think I actually prefer when it's just you with your acoustic guitar.
>
> **Sam:** Thanks! Yeah, I still play some of that stuff too
>
> **Sam:** With this band, though, we went with a style that we knew would get a record deal
>
> **Sam:** I know it's a bit commercial. But that's how you make it these days.

How you make it. Of course he was on the path to "making it." There was a reason he stopped me in my tracks on my way to do laundry years before, pulling me out of my otherwise stone-faced Sunday night ritual.

A little while later, Sam and I said our farewells and I closed my laptop, reaching down to set it back on the pink carpeted floor beside my bed. I folded my arms down in front of me and rested the side of my head on them with my eyes open as I contemplated Sam and his music, and then I sighed and smiled to myself. *One way or another, I hope he makes it.*

CHAPTER TEN

Coffee with an Old Friend

I TOOK A SEAT AT THE FAMILY COMPUTER. I had some time before my parents and I were going to sit down to dinner, so I clicked open my Gmail. It was fall 2009 now, and the Jewish holiday of Yom Kippur was to begin that evening. I had traveled from DC for a long weekend to observe the holiday, and now we were getting ready to partake in the customary large meal before the ritual fast the next day.

As I scanned my email, I saw a notification from Facebook with the subject line: "Jared Glazer sent you a message on Facebook."

I felt my breath catch in my throat. *Jared?* It was right around three years now since we had last had any contact. When he told me off at the martini event, it had felt like the end of any friendship between us, and when I saw him again at the Shabbat dinner soon after that, when we had both acted maturely, it had felt like closure. I had thought about him occasionally over the last several years, mostly if I was at a Jewish-related event where I would briefly wonder if I would run into him again. Now, I realized I didn't even know if he still lived in DC anymore.

A lot had happened in my life since I had last seen Jared. In addition to having graduated law school and taken and passed the Maryland bar exam, I had started my first job with the DC government. I had also had three more serious boyfriends during that time, none which lasted to the present. All that said and done, Jared was far from my life and my mind.

So I was startled to see a note from him. I clicked open the email and read the body of the message.

Subject: Chag Sameach

Hey Jess,

Just writing to say have an easy fast! Hope it's a meaningful holiday.

Shana Tova,
Jared

I looked at the message with its customary holiday greetings, pleasantly surprised but also perplexed. His words were casual and friendly; on the one hand, it was sweet that he had thought of me on the eve of an important and meaningful Jewish holiday, but on the other hand, I wondered how many distant friends he had sent a similar message to. I closed out my email, sighed, and rolled back the desk chair.

I got up and made my way to the front of our house and sat down on the broad, wooden staircase off the entryway, puzzling over Jared's message. Even if he sent the same thing to several others, this was Jared, reaching out over years of silence, to me, his onetime confidante, his onetime romantic interest. *Is that supposed to mean something?* I sighed and looked ahead of me through the tall, narrow windows lining the front door. I remembered sitting on the front step just outside that door with Jared all those years before when we were nineteen and he had looked into my eyes and I saw an entire future laid out for me that I was not yet ready for.

I thought about everything that had transpired with us since that time. Me breaking things off. Me trying to chase him back and soon realizing it was too hard to stay friends. Me ending our friendship and hurting his feelings. I then recalled when I had seen him most recently at the two synagogue events in DC—how he was first angry then polite. *Maybe he's just trying to be friends.* I realized that perhaps Jared was simply reaching across space and time to send a message that said, regardless of all that had happened between us, we were still friends, and given that we were both about to celebrate a solemn holiday as Jews, he wanted to send his wishes.

I walked back to the computer, sat down in the rolling chair, and slid in toward the desk. I typed a short and friendly reply to Jared and clicked send. I nodded silently to myself before shutting down the computer and standing up to make my way into our dining room for dinner.

———————

I STEPPED OUT OF THE ADJOINING BATH-room, my bare feet pressing into the pink carpet in my childhood bedroom. As I made my way toward my bed, exhausted from the day of services and fasting later followed by excessive eating, I stopped in front of the oak bookshelf on my right as something caught my eye. I glanced at the thick, tan book sitting out on the top shelf with its worn spine and corners folded back from use. It was *The Poisonwood Bible*, the book Jared had lent me all those years ago when I visited him in New York after our freshman year. After returning home, I had placed it in that very spot on the bookshelf and never touched it again. It never made it to a vertical position, filed away neatly with the other books on the shelf. Instead, it sat face up on the edge, intended to be read but never picked up again, like a frozen moment from another time, a vestige of a prior life that watched the rest of the world continue on outside the bookshelf in front of it. I picked the book up now, turning it over in my hands, and wondered if Jared had any idea that I still had it after all this time. I set it back down in its place and marveled over how quaint, innocent, and naive a reflection it was of an earlier time. So much had changed since that day at Jared's house in Queens when he had handed me the book with full trust that, someday, I would return it.

———

I OPENED MY EYES THE NEXT MORNING AND looked around my room, still lying in bed. The red numbers on the old clock radio on my nightstand read 9:28 a.m. I had fallen asleep the night before in a contemplative mood. The Yom Kippur holiday required a reflection on things you may have done wrong during the year before, including how you may have wronged others, and I had still been ruminating on this sentiment when I nodded off. I looked out at the bookshelf at the foot of my bed now, remembering *The Poisonwood Bible*.

I sighed and sank down deeper into my bed thinking of Jared's Facebook message from the day before which had, out of the blue, skipped across years of silence and landed in my inbox. I pulled the blanket up closer to my face and felt suddenly overcome with repentant emotion. I felt sorry for the way everything had transpired with Jared over the years, and in particular, anything that I had done to hurt him. I closed my eyes, remembering our last Gchat conversation right when he had moved to DC that summer more than three years before, and how he was looking to connect with friends. I had decided that I couldn't be around him anymore because I couldn't handle, all over again, having him in my life when he was with someone else. I took a deep breath, realizing I no longer felt any anger or resentment toward him for trying to stay connected with me when there were lingering feelings between us. *Maybe he's a good person who just wanted to be my friend. And I repudiated him.*

I opened my eyes, overwhelmed by the sensation that I owed Jared an apology. I realized I wanted him to know that I regretted the way things had turned out between us, and I understood that it wasn't fair that I had hurt him to protect my own feelings. And even if it was fair, I was still sorry that he ended up being hurt. I sat up on my bed, feeling a sudden and ardent desire to right this wrong from the past. I swung my blue plaid flannel-covered legs out from under the comforter so that my feet were touching the carpet. I didn't know how to begin to tell Jared how I felt via Facebook, or even in person, but I knew that whatever I did, it had to be now. I closed my eyes again. *I'm sorry, Jared. I'm sorry for the way everything transpired between us. I'm sorry I couldn't be your friend when you needed me to be there. I hope you can forgive me.*

As I said the words in my mind, in the spirit of the Yom Kippur holiday, I felt bathed in feelings of penitence toward him. I silently willed the words out into the universe in the hope that they would somehow find their way to him, wherever he was.

I took a deep breath and opened my eyes. I felt better, lighter. I had done what I needed to do to feel right and was ready to move forward into the new Jewish year. I stood up and unzipped the black suitcase that sat in the center of the floor and started to pack up my things to head back to DC.

I OPENED THE DOOR TO MY STUDIO APART-
ment in the Cleveland Park neighborhood and switched
on the light. I rolled my suitcase further into the room,
closed the door, then exhaled. It was nice to be home. I
stretched my right leg out in front of me then my left. I
had spent nearly the entire day traveling from Pennsylvania back to DC on a journey that required two different
buses. I looked at my watch now. It was just before 8:00
p.m. I thought of how refreshing the air had felt on my
skin when I had stepped out of the taxi cab moments
ago. I noticed now that all of my muscles felt tight and
achy from being cramped into a small bus seat, and I realized that I had breathed stale bus air for the majority of
the day. So, with my coat still on, I left my suitcase and
turned around and headed right back out the door of my
apartment. *I need to walk.*

I started making my way down Connecticut Avenue. I
wasn't usually out at this time during the week, especially
going the opposite direction from home, but there were
still plenty of people out and about. I decided that I would
walk down the hill just past the next metro stop in Woodley Park then turn around and head back home. It felt great
to stride one leg and then the other, getting my blood flow-
ing as I luxuriated in breathing the crisp, cool fall air into
my lungs. As my walk took on a quicker rhythm, I began to
feel my balance restoring. I continued to take brisk steps,
my hands tight in the pockets of my black wool coat. I

thought back to that morning when I had been ruminating about Jared after so long. I looked at the faces that passed me on Connecticut Avenue, and I wondered whether he still lived in DC. I didn't feel any animosity toward him anymore. It felt like I had somehow set something right in the universe with my moment of apology toward him, even though I had never said the words aloud.

A few blocks later, as I neared the Woodley Park metro station, I saw a male figure walking up the hill in the opposite direction. I recalled something that often happens to me—if I have recently seen or been thinking about someone, then I tend to see their face in others around me, and often I'll even think I'm seeing them when it's just someone with a resemblance. I don't think I would necessarily have noticed these resembling individuals but for the fact that I had that particular person on my mind. So I wasn't completely surprised when out of the corner of my eye, I saw the outline of short, curly hair on the strong, masculine build of the figure walking toward me. He reminded me of Jared, who I had just been thinking about. As he approached, I began to make out his facial features. *Wow, he really does look like Jared. How funny.* I exhaled as I walked quickly and thought with relief about how it felt like I had finally made peace with him and our past. Just as the figure was about to pass me under a street lamp, I stole a quick glance at his face to confirm that it wasn't actually Jared. I audibly gasped and stared at him in disbelief.

"Jared?" *What on earth. How . . . it IS him.*

"Oh, hey, Jess!" he replied after a brief moment of surprise from being jolted from his purposeful walk. "Long time no see! Where ya headed?"

I was so completely staggered by the fact that he was standing in front of me, as though thinking about him had literally conjured him to life before me, that I wasn't even sure what to say about why I was walking around outside at night by myself, in the opposite direction from where I lived. It almost felt as though I had willed the two of us to meet. *What do I say—I was subconsciously hoping I would run into you, even though I haven't seen you in three years and have no idea where you live?* Because I had just been thinking about him a few blocks before, and because I had thought so strongly and significantly of him that morning, it felt like any explanation that I could give as to why I was out would sound like a sham. As soon as I knew that it was him walking past, it felt like the only reason that I had taken a walk that night was so that we could run into each other, at this spot, in this moment.

After we parted ways three years before, I had occasionally imagined running into Jared years later if we were both still living in DC. In my mind, I would be at some sort of Israel, Jewish, or political-related conference. I would be attending a plenary session in a large ballroom with broad, sparkling chandeliers scattered on the ceiling above the endless rows of stiff, gray hotel chairs. Walking in a black sheath dress and smart black heels with a tasteful pearl necklace and matching earrings, I would choose a seat in the middle of a row and set my black professional-looking bag beside me on a chair. I would suddenly see Jared walking toward a seat a few rows ahead of me. He would have the same close-cropped, light curly hair, and he would look important, dressed in a crisp white dress shirt and gray slacks. Our eyes would meet, and we would walk back out to the aisle to politely connect and share our mutual passion for whatever Israel, Jewish, or political-related issue the conference was about.

We would then sit back down in two seats next to each other and continue to catch up. He would have gotten over whatever had happened between us so many years back, and I would have too. We would be fully grown adults, more mature versions of ourselves capable of a conversation unconnected to the drama of our shared past. We would make plans to grab lunch together after the session. Maybe we would even fall in love with each other again over that lunch.

But here Jared was, standing in front of me now, outside the metro station on Connecticut Avenue, in the darkness of a fall night. I eventually managed to find my words.

"I just got back from Pennsylvania and needed to get out for some air after the trip. I was about to head back home."

Jared gestured up the hill. "You're that way? I live a block up from here, but if you want I can walk with you toward home for a few minutes before I head back."

I nodded, and we began to walk side by side up the street in the brisk air. The dry leaves crackled under our feet as we made our way below a canopy of tree branches that still held many of their full but drying yellow, red, and orange leaves. As we talked, I learned that he lived just between the Woodley Park and Cleveland Park metro stops, minutes from my apartment.

"I'm surprised we haven't run into each other yet," I said, mystified.

I looked at Jared's profile as he walked next to me, remembering that less than twelve hours before, I had essentially wished for the ability to apologize to him for what had happened between us years before. And now he was next to me, walking with me toward home. *Holy shit. I could apologize to him for real.*

I realized if I didn't say it now, I might never have another chance, and I didn't want to waste this strange opportunity that felt like it had been given to me. At a brief lull in our conversation, I turned to look at him.

"By the way, can I just say quickly that I'm sorry for the way everything went down with us when you first moved to DC? I feel bad that I sort of ditched you as a friend, but I was just doing what I needed to do at the time." The words flew out of my mouth.

"Oh, no worries," he said, and then turned to me and grinned. "I'm sorry too. Ancient history."

We were both silent for a few moments as we faced forward again, our feet periodically crunching on the leaves below us. I watched the headlights of several cars pass us by, their beams forming mini tunnels of light in the clear darkness of the night.

After a few more minutes of idle catching up, Jared needed to turn and head back. We agreed to stay in touch and get a drink sometime. After he left to make his way back down the hill toward his apartment, I continued to walk back up the street toward my own. I shook my head in disbelief. *Did that really just happen?*

———————

I PULLED OPEN THE DOOR TO OPEN CITY, A popular coffeehouse right at the Metro stop in Woodley Park. It was 8:30 p.m. on a Sunday, but the small, warmly lit establishment was practically bursting at the seams with convivial patrons eating, drinking, and laughing. I stood inside and looked around for Jared, ignoring the glances that the eager and overworked-looking hostesses were shooting my way. I didn't see him and quickly felt myself surrounded on all sides and pushed back toward the door by a tidal wave of college students that had just charged inside. I carefully dodged some arms and handbags and made my way through the partially open door and back into the night. Spotting an available bench near the restaurant's patio, I quickly sat down before someone else did.

I took in a large mouthful of the brisk late fall air and exhaled, then crossed my right leg over my left and began jiggling my foot anxiously. I periodically looked up to see if Jared had arrived. Even though it was somewhat cool outside, I was grateful for the fresh air. I took another full breath and sighed. *Just chill.* I knew that when he got there, I couldn't be anxious. I couldn't be too excited to see him; I had to be cool. I truly didn't know what to expect from our coffee. The few minutes that we had chatted outside the Woodley Park metro when we ran into each other weeks before were so brief and cursory; I still had no idea how well we would get along anymore, if at all. I also didn't know how I felt about him, romantically or otherwise.

I knew at a minimum that I had recently reconnected with a person who, at one time, was important to me, and there's a certain comfort to be had in spending time with someone who truly knows you. At least the last that I had checked, Jared was one of the few people that I felt I could put into that category. *So that's it then. I'm just catching up with an old friend. Nothing to be nervous about.*

But deep down, beneath my attempt to play it cool, I knew that there was a tiny shard of curious excitement that I couldn't deny. I was single. Was Jared single? Was THIS finally the moment in our lives when we would cross paths at the right time with no inhibitions, no fears, and no one else in the picture? Years ago we had paddled away from each other in the same ocean. Maybe now we were both on land, walking on different paths, tracing opposite sides of the same circle and about to meet. Instead of simply passing by each other on the course of our respective lives with possible acknowledgment, maybe a nod of the head before continuing on our own routes in different directions, maybe this time it would be different. Maybe we were actually about to meet in the same place, at the same time. At the *right* time. And maybe for the first time we would stop then continue forward in the same direction. I thought back again to when I passed Jared on the sidewalk that dark fall night after Yom Kippur several weeks before. We were walking in opposite directions, but he walked briefly out of his way, in my direction, toward home.

I actively worked to suppress that fragment of excitement that I felt for what could be because I still didn't know what was. I tried to temper my expectations as best as I could. *Coffee with an old friend. What's not enjoyable about coffee with an old friend?*

I took a few more deep breaths of the cool evening air and looked back at the door to the restaurant just in time to see Jared, in a black leather jacket, stepping back outside to look for me. He smiled that giant blinded-by-the-light smile that could knock an innocent bystander to the ground, but for the genuineness that sparkled from his light blue-gray eyes. *Jared.* It had been so long since I had spent time with him, or even thought about him for an extended period that it felt nice to simply be in the same space, breathing the same air, looking each other in the eyes. In that moment, it didn't even really matter what happened next since I was already calmed by his presence.

At the same time, though, I quickly noticed that physically, Jared looked slightly different than I had remembered. When I had run into him walking down Connecticut Avenue, it was dark and I was surprised, so I didn't really get to take him in. Now, I couldn't figure out exactly what had changed. I didn't think I remembered him putting any type of product in his short curls in the past, and now that I thought about it, his hair seemed a bit longer. I realized that it was possible he could simply never actually match up to the idealized version of who he was in my memory—that boy from a formative period during my teen years who I maybe liked and who I maybe missed my chance with. Who maybe still liked me, too.

We shared a quick embrace before Jared pointed to the door to the restaurant with his thumb.

"Should we try and grab a table? Looks packed."

I nodded. Inspecting Jared more closely now, I suddenly understood at least part of why he looked different to me. Despite the level of contentment that I felt by simply having him look at me and smile, all at once I glimpsed him within the context of his surroundings, standing outside Open City on an autumn night in DC. Enough time had passed that I was able to see him objectively somehow, separate from the image of him etched into my mind from the past. As I looked at him, I simply saw a dorky young professional Jewish guy living in DC like so many others. As he came into clearer relief for me with the backdrop of this city that I had come to know so well while he and I had gone our separate ways, somehow he didn't stand out to me anymore, as though the magic had disappeared into the dark night. I felt a pang of disappointment tinged with a slight sadness. I blinked and tried to stay emotionally neutral. We hadn't even gone inside the restaurant yet.

Once we made our way in, we were seated at a table for two near the door. *Like a date.* Jared slid into the chair backing up to the window at the small table, so I took the other one facing him. I truly had no idea whether or not this was a date or whether I even wanted it to be. Regardless, as I sat down and saw Jared across the table from me, I was glad to be there with him. Despite my initial impression of him outside the restaurant, it still felt poetic to me that after our romance so long ago, when we were still teenagers, here we sat sharing a table together while living in the same city nine years later. When the waitress approached, he ordered a beer, and I asked for a soy cappuccino.

"So you're the DD?" Jared joked.

I chuckled. "I just know it's going to be a busy work week, and I feel even one drink the next day, so it's better to just not."

Jared smiled. "What, you can't write policy hungover?"

I smiled and shrugged.

When the waitress returned with our drinks, Jared poured the golden yellow liquid from his beer bottle into the tall, fluted glass next to it. I watched a thin layer of foam rise to the top as the glass filled. I picked up my cappuccino, served in one of Open City's standard large white coffee mugs, a perfect layer of white-feathered light brown foam on top. There were two animal crackers next to the spoon on the saucer below, an Open City trademark. I cradled the mug in both of my hands, enjoying its warmth before taking a sip. The frothy liquid was nearly scalding hot but still rich and earthy on my tongue. I looked over my mug and across the table at Jared. There was something else about him that seemed changed, but I couldn't place what it was. Maybe it was just that he was several years older and maybe slightly more mature. He was still strikingly good-looking, and he also seemed several shades more confident than I had remembered.

"So tell me about school," I said.

I had learned that he was getting a graduate degree in international relations here in DC.

He smiled. "I love it. It's a lot of work, but it's almost done. Luckily I'll be doing a lot of traveling with the program, both this winter and then again in the spring. One of the trips is to China, so I'm pretty excited about that."

I smiled back. "Sounds great."

He took a long drink from his beer glass then looked at me. "And what about you—tell me about that DC government job. Kicking ass and taking names?"

I laughed. "Something like that. It's not exactly what I want to do long term."

As we talked, I tried to get a read on how Jared was approaching the evening. He seemed to be treating it like a friendly drink with nary a romantic vibe, so I mimicked that sentiment, holding back any flirtation or display of specific interest if it was not coming from the other direction. I also still hadn't decided whether I felt any interest at all. I took another sip of my cappuccino.

"It's hard to believe it's been, what, nine years since that Israel trip when we first met?" I mused.

Jared shook his head. "I know, right?" Then he grinned. "When did we get so old?"

With some discouragement, I noticed that our conversation felt a bit surface-level and stunted to me. While we were having a perfectly friendly exchange, I kept searching for the connection that we used to have—the smart, flirty banter, the raw openness that came from feeling close, comfortable, and alike. I kept coming up empty though, and I began to realize that it did not actually feel as though we were connecting particularly well at all. As we continued talking, I studied Jared and realized that although we were sitting at a small table in a cozy restaurant merely feet from each other, he felt farther away from me than he ever had.

I tried to find something, anything, to connect us, to bring us back.

"You know, there was something that you said to me a long time ago that I really liked, that actually stuck with me. I still think about it sometimes."

Jared made a funny face. "Uh-oh. I'm afraid to know what I said now."

I gave a small laugh. "No, it's not bad. So we were talking about how we both hated when people talked about other people behind their backs, like based on their appearance or something, and you said it really bothered you because someone's looks were often something that they couldn't control."

Before I could continue, Jared scoffed, "Wow, did I really say that? I don't remember that at all. That's kind of a weird and dorky thing to say. I'm not sure if I would even agree with that now. But OK, if you're giving me credit for saying it, then sure, I'll take the credit." He smiled.

I gave him a small smile and looked down at my cappuccino as I felt my heart sink slightly. When we had that conversation as college freshmen, it had meant something to me that we related in that way, and I had held onto it years later as some of the evidence of our unique connection and alikeness. That tiny sliver of hope I had felt while sitting outside earlier before Jared arrived was slowly beginning to dissipate. It was becoming clear to me that the Jared I knew from back then, the version of him that I carried in the back of my mind for so long, was not the same Jared that now sat across from me tonight. Though nearly a decade had passed and we had grown through our twenties separately, my memories of him hadn't changed, and only now did I realize how sorely out of date and naive they were.

As the image of Jared in my mind began to erode into a closer representation of reality, it was as though a large multi-colored balloon that I had so hopefully carried to the table with me that night, clutching onto its white ribbon like a child, had suddenly become untied. The air began slowly leaking out as it swirled back and forth in the air in front of us, finally spinning out of control before making its ultimate escape and shooting through the restaurant door, just as a twenty-something man in a backward baseball cap opened it up to step inside. And then the balloon was gone, into the dark night, into oblivion, the white ribbon now coiled up on the floor, a remnant of a moment passed.

I took a large sip of my cappuccino then set the mug back down in its saucer and leaned back in my chair, looking at Jared again. *I am not attracted to him at all.* Although he was still easy on the eyes, the person that I had felt so deeply connected to and attracted to at one point in time did not appear to exist anymore. Looking at him now, I didn't notice kindness and warmth emanating from his eyes anymore so much as I recognized a newfound arrogance. Maybe that was what I had perceived at the beginning of the evening that I couldn't put my finger on. I felt slightly sad as I realized I wasn't sure whether or not we were even going to be friends.

While I recognized that Jared had changed, I also knew that I wasn't necessarily the same person that he had known back then, either. As I saw him with clearer eyes than ever before, at the same time, I saw myself acutely in comparison. It was an older version of me that looked at him now across my soy cappuccino, one that had tasted love and hurt. One that had learned, and one that had settled into who she was in her adult life and knew what she wanted in a partner. The lack of chemistry that I felt with Jared now reminded me of a sentiment I had experienced many times on a first date, when you suddenly know that there's not going to be a second one. That moment when you realize with disappointment but complete confidence that you probably will never see that person again after that night.

When Jared got up to use the restroom, I thought back for a moment to that bright, sunny day in New York City when we sat on the large rocks together in Central Park. We were so happy to simply be sitting close together for the first time after years of instant messaging and slowly-igniting intrigue. He told me then how he felt awkward telling his friends about me because he would say in the same breath how great I was but also how I was so much like him. And now, here we were, two divergent people who had some things in common, once.

After Jared returned and we talked more about his upcoming travel plans, I recognized another chasm between us. As he spoke, I saw the same ardent thirst for life, adventure, and newness that he had had when we were nineteen. I, though, felt like I had grown to a place where I craved more stability. I could tell that Jared sought to attach himself to someone or something exciting, to be part of an adventure. I was happy where I was. It was now evident to me that we weren't even seeking the same things from life at this point in time.

I knew that part of why Jared had been so interested in me during our freshman year of college was that he liked the chase. I was this girl living hours away in Pennsylvania who he had to seek out, to pursue. There was mystery and intrigue. At the time, I liked the chase just as much as he did. I was also just as restless and eager as he was to explore as much of the world as I possibly could, to see and experience everything, because why sit still, why be complacent? I recognized that in Jared then, and I saw now that at least that part of him had remained exactly the same. As I comprehended this, cradling my cappuccino in my hands while still listening to Jared talk, all at once I knew that I was no longer that person whose sense of adventure sparked Jared's in the way that he needed it to in order to hold his interest. As a result, I knew then that Jared didn't like me either, at least in that way. *He still needs a girl that he can chase.*

I instantly felt lighter sitting at the table. The realization that not only was Jared not the one for me but that I was not the one for him was cathartic. I watched him wipe his mouth with a small white cocktail napkin after finishing the last swig from his beer glass. *Maybe we can be friends after all.* It felt like the air was truly, finally clear between us. Because I knew there couldn't possibly be anything romantic with us—and I imagined he felt something similar—there was room for friendship. I set down my empty mug, feeling at ease and smiling the largest smile I had all night.

We walked back outside together after paying the check.

"Well, let's definitely stay in touch," I said as I buttoned up my coat. And I meant it.

He gave me a genuine grin in return. "For sure."

We shared a comfortable, friendly hug, and then I watched him walk toward the crosswalk in the direction of his apartment. I smiled to myself as I continued up the street toward my own, the collar of my black wool coat pulled high around my neck to block out the crispness in the air. My steps felt light on the pavement as I walked. Ever since my sophomore year after I had broken things off with Jared, I had always wondered, at least in the back of my mind, whether I had made a mistake, whether I had simply been scared away from something potentially real when I was too young to understand it. But I knew now that even if we had truly gotten together at that time, we wouldn't have stayed together, or ended up together. This was an easy, comfortable kind of certainty, the first certitude that I had felt about Jared since I noticed him across the Shabbat dinner tables in Israel so many years before and knew I had to meet him. I sighed, feeling warmed by the notion. *Closure.*

———————

WHEN I OPENED THE FRONT DOOR OF MY apartment building to walk outside, I saw that someone had plowed the walkway at one point, but my feet still sank into a few inches of fresh snow. On either side of me, the path was lined with two neat walls of icy whiteness several feet high. Even though DC was still recovering from the "Snowpocalypse" which happened back in December, the local media outlets had dubbed this February storm "Snowmageddon." It was nearly impossible to get around the city because no one was driving on the roads and all of the public transportation had been shut down.

About a half an hour earlier, Jared had sent me a message on Gchat.

> **Jared:** Enjoying the snow?
> **me:** Well, there's literally nowhere I can go, so...I guess?
> **Jared:** I hear you. Been home for the last 24 hours
> **me:** Yeah. It's nuts out there
> **me:** Hey, we live close. Want to meet up?
> **Jared:** Sure
> **Jared:** Anything open?
> **me:** Let me find out...

I made a few phone calls and learned that the neighborhood Irish pub, Ireland's Four Green Fields, was miraculously open on this white-out night, so I had bundled up and was headed there now to meet Jared. I slowly made my way toward Connecticut Avenue in tall black boots that covered my jeans, the only pair I had been able to locate with something on the bottom resembling traction. Before I reached the main thoroughfare, I had to trudge through several yards of unplowed sidewalk, my feet sinking through stiffly packed snow that rose up to my knees. I stopped suddenly when I realized that I was just about to enter the empty, snow-covered street, barely distinguishable from the white-blanketed sidewalks that lined either side. There were no car tracks on the street, only fresh snow. I didn't even see anyone else outside.

The deep layer of whiteness that coated the street and enshrouded the city sparkled beneath the soft amber beams of the streetlights that shone above from their silver poles against the otherwise dark sky. I looked up toward the lights and could see large, nickel-sized flakes still falling slowly. I paused for a moment to take in the resplendent scene. It was a surreal sight for an otherwise bustling artery of the city, now quieted by the simple, silent beauty of a soft white cloak come alive by still falling snow. I trekked diagonally across the open expanse of street toward the bar with no perception of where a crosswalk would have even been. It felt like I had the Cleveland Park neighborhood to myself.

Approaching the bar, I thought about how grateful I was that Jared and I had successfully stayed in touch as friends. We were more on the casual friends end of the spectrum than close friends; we invited each other to various group events and chatted online occasionally now. He had attended a Chanukah party at my apartment recently where he actually connected with Lauren, a friend of one of my law school friends, and when he asked for her number later, I had very willingly connected the two of them. *How cool would it be if they ended up together and it was my party where they first met?*

I found Jared inside the bar, already sitting on a bench at one of the wooden tables. I looked around, surprised to see a handful of other patrons inside. When I approached the table, I saw that he was on the phone.

"Sorry," he mouthed to me silently with wide eyes as I sat down across from him.

I took off my coat, which sparkled with tiny wet droplets now, and slung it behind me on the wooden chair. I scanned the laminated drink menu in front of me.

A few minutes later, Jared set his now-darkened cell phone on the table between us.

"Sorry about that. It was Samantha, my ex. She calls me sometimes, and I just sort of have to listen."

Figures. There's always someone. Always some drama.

"Interesting," I said pointedly. "Even though you guys are broken up, you don't mind that she calls you?"

Jared smiled. "Well, she's sort of, well . . . special. It's really easy to set her off. I know it's helpful for her to talk to me, and I know it's just easier." I nodded slowly as he continued. "So when she's upset, I feel like it's the nice thing to do, and I really don't mind."

I thought to myself how he really did not seem to mind and seemed to actually enjoy it.

Jared shook his head. "Yeah, she was a unique one. Very controlling. We would be having sex and all of a sudden she would get really angry at me and say, 'Are you thinking about someone else right now? I know you are!'" He took a sip from the beer bottle in front of him and grinned. "And the truth is, I actually was."

I gave him a nod-shrug while thinking to myself how distressing it would be to be in a relationship with someone who held on so closely to past connections while also continuing to flirt with and charm new girls in the present. I had been on the periphery of some of those relationships, and I had also nearly been his girlfriend while he still held onto other girls from his past. I was glad I wasn't in a relationship with Jared. I was also gratified, though, to have a friend to sit with on a lonely, snowy night.

"Did you ever end up going out with Lauren again?" I asked, remembering that they had a first date several weeks back.

Jared shook his head slowly in disappointment. "We had a great date, and she was honest with me afterward. She told me she ended up getting serious with someone else she had started dating just before me, so she had to break it off." He took another sip of his beer before setting it back down on a round cardboard coaster. "It's OK though because of Naomi."

I furrowed my brow and cocked my head slightly. "Naomi?"

"Yeah." He smiled broadly. "I knew her from BU, and I would have loved to have dated her, but we were both in relationships at the time. We've been talking a LOT recently. Only online, because she lives in Shanghai."

I nodded and smiled, intrigued.

"I'll be traveling in China over spring break next month, and I've made plans to extend my trip so I could meet her in Shanghai."

I took a sip from the large plastic water glass that had been set in front of me, ice bobbing against my top lip. *This sounds like classic Jared.*

"Awesome!" I said.

He was beaming now. "And if that visit goes well, I think this could be pretty serious. As I was just saying to a friend of mine the other day, I could marry the shit out of this girl." His eyes sparkled now.

I kept smiling but was a bit surprised by the statement. *Marry.* I thought his comment was curious since it had been mere weeks before that he had been telling me how interested in Lauren he was in a way that appeared to be serious. He had also shown genuine disappointment as he told me moments before that Lauren didn't want to go out with him again. I was most taken aback by Jared's statement, though, because I realized that in all the time I had known him, I had never actually heard him refer to a girl he was interested in in the context of marriage, particularly so early on. *Marry.* I didn't think I had ever even heard him say the word before. His small boat that I had jumped out of so long ago was back in the water again, headed straight to Shanghai, and it was evident that he couldn't wait to pull Naomi inside. And if Jared had his way, she would be the last and final occupant of the seat that I had left behind as they rowed off into the sunset together, forever.

———

I TOOK A BITE OF MY PEANUT BUTTER COV-ered whole wheat bagel then set it back down on the plate as I clicked into my Gmail. I was enjoying a lazy Saturday morning in my apartment. Suddenly I saw a chat message pop up from Jared.

> **Jared:** Heya
> **me:** Hey! Back in the states?
> **Jared:** Unfortunately, yes.
> **me:** What does that mean?
> **Jared:** Just had a whirlwind trip with Naomi.
> **me:** Was it everything you hoped, and more? :)
> **Jared:** Very much so.
> **Jared:** It went as well as I could have hoped. She's my girlfriend now =).
> **Jared:** At the moment, I'm making plans to move to Shanghai after graduation.
> **me:** Wow! That's amazing!

We chatted for a few more minutes before I signed off. I took another bite of my bagel before chasing it down with a sip of black coffee from a large Starbucks mug with a London motif on the outside. I looked down at the white Ikea desk in front of me, a few errant neon Post-it Notes with reminders scattered on its surface in front of where my silver MacBook sat. *Wow. He IS going to marry the shit out of her.* I thought about how, from everything I knew about Jared, Naomi seemed perfect for him. She had the sense of adventure that I knew would appease his perennial craving; she represented the end of a global chase, the ultimate chase, the end of which was lifetime partnership. His ardent pursuit of her reminded me of when he had chased me, on a smaller scale, so many years before as freshmen in college. This culmination of Jared's romantic trajectory made sense to me, and I felt genuinely happy for him because I knew that where he and I each were now, in the present, was where we were supposed to be.

CHAPTER ELEVEN

You Found Me Across Time and Space

I SANK DOWN INTO OUR TAN FAUX SUEDE couch, emotionally exhausted. It was the summer of 2011, and I shared a tiny one-bedroom condo in the not-yet-redeveloped Southwest Waterfront neighborhood of DC with my boyfriend of about a year, Evan. He was four years my junior, twenty-three to my twenty-seven, which hadn't mattered in the beginning. As of late, however, our relationship was beginning to wear thin and was showing definite signs of impermanence. We would fight then make up, and then we'd forget about the fight. Rinse, repeat. Lately, often. The fights were always very dramatic—occasionally involving tears in a crowded bar—and I was often able to see the ludicrousness of what was going on even when I was in the midst of it. These conflicts always felt unnecessary, and a waste of everyone's time and energy. Of all of my energy. Lately, when I was away from Evan, I often wondered whether he was the right person for me, and I had started to confide this to friends and family. When I was with him, though, it was easy to forget the doubts and keep on keeping on, until the same thing would happen yet again.

It was a Saturday night now, and I was eminently grateful that Evan had gone out with some friends, so I had the condo to myself. I relaxed back into the couch, my socked feet folded under me, relishing the quiet as I sat alone in the space. After a moment, I reached next to a pile of brown throw pillows for the remote then absent-mindedly clicked on the TV.

My thoughts were elsewhere as the large screen in front of me lit up with a commercial. It didn't even matter what I was looking at; I was simply relieved to have some time in my own head without any conflicting emotions . . . without Evan. I saw quick shots of people engaged in various activities flash across the screen, and then I was suddenly jolted out of my thoughts by the music playing in the background. The pop-y, computer-generated, electronic sounds rang familiar to me, but I couldn't place them. A soft voice began singing now. *I know that voice.* All at once, everything came back to me. The pale skin, the cloud of dark unruly hair as he sat on the chilly floor of our dorm hallway in Chinatown, quietly singing with his guitar. *It's Sam.*

I felt my face flush at the recognition. I thought of his face peeking through the crack in his dorm room door with his hair rumpled from sleep as I handed him my email address on a neon blue Post-it Note. My mind went next to our date in the East Village when I was having a great time until all at once I felt intimidated, scared, and unable to move forward. Then I remembered how, years later, he had sent me this very song through Gchat when I chatted with him on my laptop at my parents' house. I thought about how he told me he had recorded an album. I stared at the screen now, my mouth agape, and saw a Verizon logo flash across the TV just before the commercial ended. Moments before, the ad had meant nothing to me, now all of a sudden, it was everything. *He made it.*

Another commercial had started to play, but as I gaped at the TV, I looked right through it, still ruminating on the pleasant surprise of hearing Sam's voice when I least expected it. I snuggled deeper into the couch and thought about how when I first met him outside the laundry room at NYU, I was stuck in place, stuck in front of him in the hallway because I couldn't stop listening to his enchanting voice. Then we went on our date, a real date, a thing that could have been the beginning of a genuine something, and I couldn't move forward. I was, again, stuck. I was stuck outside the bakery that night, stuck in time, stuck in fear. And now, eight years later, I was stuck yet again. Here I sat, lost, sinking, anchored in this condo, moored to this relationship. Suddenly here was Sam's voice again, unknowingly singing to me, across space and time. Hearing his voice touched me and moved me from my fixed spot on the couch, my immobile place in life.

I thought about how he might have been singing to me that day back in college while I was doing my laundry.

"So why don't you . . . take off your shoes. . . . " I would never know for sure, but I liked to think that he was. I smiled, appreciating how unbeknownst to him, years later, he was still singing to me. And his voice was just what I needed to hear at this juncture to connect me to who I was in a different place and time.

———

AS THE ESCALATOR CARRIED ME UP TO GROUND level, I stepped onto the sidewalk, turned to my left, and walked toward the Acre 121 bar. I took quick steps, shedding my workday behind with each stride. The early December air was cold, but it wasn't worth bundling up for the half-a-block walk in the Columbia Heights neighborhood of DC. It was a Thursday night, and I was on my way to meet a few friends. The past several months, during the fall of 2011, I had played in a social bocce ball league, which played on a court on the rooftop of an apartment building right off the Columbia Heights metro stop. Over the course of the season, our team had won several gift certificates to Acre 121, located just underneath the apartment building, and tonight was the night we planned to meet to cash them in.

My recent ex, Evan, was still technically on my bocce team, but we had worked out a sort of unspoken arrangement to show up during different weeks of games, and I knew he wasn't planning to attend the happy hour tonight. I looked at my watch. It was 6:45 p.m., and I was still in the midst of an insane work week. It didn't feel like the best night to be out, but I wanted to support my friend from law school, Kirsten, who had organized the happy hour. *I'll just have a drink or two then head home.*

I arrived at the bar just as Kirsten was approaching from the other direction on the sidewalk.

"Hey!" we said to each other before sharing a quick hug.

After we pushed through the glass doors to go inside, we saw Esteban, a friend I had met through my younger brother Mike, already seated at the bar with a beer in front of him.

"Hey girrrrls!" Esteban said excitedly in slightly accented English.

The doors swung closed behind us, and I felt the warmth of the heat inside the bar. As I saw the glow of twinkling Christmas lights strung festively around the room and heard Esteban's warm welcome, I felt embraced in a sanctuary far from the office I had walked out of less than an hour before. I was glad I had come.

A little while later we were joined by Clarissa, a friend of Evan's who I had gotten to know. Kirsten, Esteban, and I were standing close to the bar, our winter coats stacked on a bar stool in front of us. After Clarissa tossed her coat onto the pile, Kirsten looked at us and raised her voice slightly.

"OK, time for shots! We've got some bocce league money to burn."

Moments later, there were four tiny glasses in front of us filled with clear liquid. We toasted, drank down our shots, then all laughed as Esteban chugged an Irish Car Bomb immediately afterward. I felt the alcohol warm my body as it went down, and I knew it was going to be a fun night.

The four of us stayed by the bar talking and acting silly together for a solid couple of hours. The window during which I had planned to leave had already closed by the time Kirsten suggested heading to the restaurant next door for another drink. I peeked at my watch, and for a brief moment, thought about having to wake up early for a busy day tomorrow. Then I looked up at the eager faces of Kirsten, Clarissa, and Esteban waiting to see what my response was going to be. We were having so much fun, and I didn't want the night to end yet.

"OK, I'll go for a little bit," I decided. "Let's do it."

By the time we had settled into a deep red vinyl booth next door with food and drinks set in front of us, in this new environment with slightly brighter lights, significantly less people, and softer music, we found ourselves tiring out and our night began to wind down. I dunked the plastic straw into my water glass a few times, watching the ice bob around.

"Should we ask for the check?" I offered.

Just then, I glanced over absentmindedly at the booth to my right, across a small open aisle. I hadn't noticed until just then that a group of three men had sat down there who were now talking and laughing loudly. I heard someone speaking in slightly accented English, and I noticed that it was the man sitting at the edge of the booth and facing in my direction. I picked up my water glass now and took a sip from the straw, then glanced over at the man again. He looked familiar. Dark hair, dark stubble. Deep brown eyes. *Wow, he really looks like Avi.*

I remembered the last time I had seen Avi, literally crossing paths at that massive event in Israel seven years ago. Camp, where I had met him, was nine years ago. As I responded to something Esteban said, my ears were still perked toward the table across the aisle. When the man at the end said something to his friends, I heard the accent again and realized he actually sounded like Avi also. *Is it possible?* I shook my head and looked down, distractedly moving the straw around in my water glass again and trying not to reveal to my friends at the table with me that I had noticed anything in particular to my right.

Our server had already set the check down on our table, so I tossed my credit card onto the pile that had quickly formed on top of it. I was feeling quite tired now and ready to hail a cab and call it a night. I snuck one more glance at the man at the table to the right that looked like Avi. Someone in his booth had just said something funny, and he and the third man broke out into hearty laughter in response. My eyes lingered on him just in time to see his face illuminated by a huge smile that dazzled as brightly as the playful glint in his deep brown eyes. I knew that face instantly. I squinted and then stared.

Without saying anything to my friends, I slowly slid out of the booth, walked across the aisle, then stopped so I was standing right over this man. I leaned down closer to catch his attention.

"Avi?"

He looked back up at me with searching eyes. There was no doubt in my mind now that it was him.

"It's Jessica . . . from Camp Laurelwood?" I watched as the recognition softened his face and he blinked.

"Oh, wow, Jessica!" Looking mystified, he stood up so he could face me.

As I watched Avi standing across from me, I understood why I had decided to come out that night despite all circumstances pointing me not to, and why I had stayed out and even came to the restaurant afterward, all in spite of the fact that I so desperately needed every minute of sleep I could squeeze in before facing a pile of work on my desk early the next morning. It had all directed me to this moment. I shook my head, disbelieving the sight in front of me. Avi in DC, in my city. *How was this even possible?*

"Are you visiting DC?" I asked him, internally marveling that I would chance upon meeting him this way.

"I live here," he said. "For about four years now."

I explained how I had been living here since college. As we talked excitedly, one of the men from his booth snapped a picture. Immediately posted to Facebook with the caption "Awkward moment for Avi," the image shows both of us gesticulating wildly, amazed by the fact that we were both in the same restaurant that night. At the moment the scene was captured, I am gesturing toward Avi, almost pointing, while he is holding both hands slightly inward, fingers spread out, as if he were offering some sort of explanation for whatever imaginary accusation I was throwing at him; together we looked like an old married couple having a squabble.

Eventually our respective friends grew impatient with us talking while standing in between the booths, so Avi and I exchanged numbers and decided to catch up more another time. I went back to my seat to three friends, eyebrows raised and waiting for an explanation, so I shared a very abbreviated version of how I knew Avi. Sitting back down I still felt somewhat in shock from having seen him. It was unexpected but still pleasant somehow. Any animus I had felt toward him from years ago had now long since faded. At this moment, it was simply enjoyable to see a face I knew from the past, from a faraway place. First at Camp Laurelwood in Madison, Connecticut, and then so briefly in a crowded building in Jerusalem, and now, in the Columbia Heights neighborhood of Washington, DC, at the tail end of an already pleasantly surprising Thursday night. There he was, again.

———

IT WAS A FRIGID DECEMBER NIGHT AS I walked down New Hampshire Avenue to meet Avi. After some texting, we had agreed to get together for drinks at the Bier Baron Tavern near Dupont Circle on this Wednesday night. As I walked past several orderly row houses, picking up my pace in an effort to stay warm, I realized I had no idea what was going to happen once we met up. *Was this a catch-up as friends? Was this a date?* I didn't even know if Avi was single, though the vibe both when I ran into him at the restaurant and over text had certainly seemed that way. I had very recently started seeing someone that I was excited about, but we were very far from anything that could be considered exclusive, so I was technically single, too.

Running into Avi again had felt crazy, surreal, and serendipitous, but I had no expectations about where we might go from here. Although we had both lived and grown in the intervening years, it was impossible to forget that he had let me down more than once in the past. I tried to keep my mind clear and open as I slowly approached the bar since I truly did not know where Avi was going to be coming from. For my part, I was just curious, really. Why had we reconnected again? *Would we talk about the past? Does he even remember the past?*

Just as I crossed the street and walked closer to the bar, I saw Avi approaching at the same time from the sidewalk. He was wearing a long, professional-looking black winter coat, and overall appeared to be a grown man, a long way removed from the twenty-three-year-old version of him that I remembered from camp. But I knew we were both a long way removed from that time, from those people. As our eyes met, his face broke out into his trademark wide smile.

"Hey!" he said warmly.

"Hey," I said back, meeting his grin.

We hugged briefly before stepping inside the bar to seek warmth.

Given that it was a weeknight, I wasn't surprised to see that it was sparsely populated inside. We were seated at a small table against a wall in a little room off to the left that I had never been inside before. We had this space to ourselves.

As we took off our coats and hung them over our chairs, I said, "It's so funny seeing you; it's been so long."

When I spoke, I realized I was slightly nervous. So much time had passed since I had seen or talked to him before our spontaneous run-in in Columbia Heights. I didn't even know who he had grown up to become, and he didn't know anything about me anymore, either. After a waiter came in to take our drink order, Avi smiled at me, his eyes sparkling under the warm lights of our small room.

"I can't believe we ran into each other. It is such a small world. So what do you do in DC?"

As we caught up, I watched him across the table from me. His face was as I remembered it, the brown stubble forming a beard and mustache around his mouth, short brown hair spiked up a bit in the front. His familiar features showed some weathering from the years since I had seen him up close. I noticed some small, deep wrinkles around his eyes when he smiled that I did not remember from before. He told me about how, soon after camp, when he ended up working at Hillel, the Jewish center at the University of Arizona, he met a woman there who eventually became his wife. For a moment, I remembered calling Avi from outside my NYU dorm during my senior year after we had run into each other in Israel. I thought of how he had seemed distant and uninterested in spending too much time talking to me. *It makes sense now.*

I glanced down at Avi's hands and noticed that he was not wearing a wedding ring, so I figured there might be more to the story. I sipped my drink and listened as he went on to explain how his marriage happened quickly because he was going to have to go back to Israel otherwise. So, he and his girlfriend had gotten married to stay together, then it didn't end up lasting.

As he told me this story, I could see how the years and his experiences had aged his face, and the wrinkles by his eyes held meaning now. His deep, arresting brown eyes still had that special light in them that I remembered from years before, but it shone differently now. The glint of mischievousness, humor, and wonder about the world had been replaced by a more mature glow that retained some of its original playfulness but was now also tinged with a hint of wistfulness for a simpler, more carefree time.

Avi was still attractive, but interestingly, he was not as captivating as I remembered. This was not due to age or because he looked different; I recognized that it was simply because back then, during our camp days, he had felt so special to me, a twenty-three-year-old Israeli man compared to the nineteen-year-old American girl that I was. Now it felt like we were in parity, sitting together at a table in DC, a city where we both lived and worked. He was thirty-two now, and I was twenty-eight, and it seemed as though we could be any other two people in the city, except we just happened to have known each other once, a long time ago.

I watched Avi take a sip from the straw in his tall, narrow glass before setting it down and looking at me. He took an audible deep breath before speaking.

"So, I think . . . I'm supposed to be apologizing to you for something, aren't I? I can't remember exactly what for, to be completely honest, but I feel like I owe you an apology." He smiled at me sheepishly. "Am I right?"

My breath caught in my throat for a second. My mind flashed back to nine years before, laying in my bunk at Camp Laurelwood while everyone else was asleep as I listened to Avi and Orly whisper goodnight to each other outside. I remembered the sound of Avi walking away, back to his bunk, back into the night. *Crunnnch, crunnnch, crunnnnch.* I sighed as I recalled how his feet on the gravel crushed me that night like the small rocks underneath the soles of his shoes.

I let go of the straw I had been twirling in my drink and looked directly at him, my face entirely serious. "Yeah, I think you do."

His abashed smile disappeared and his face was solemn now also. "Well," he said, as he fixed his deep brown eyes on me, a new gravity cast over them. "I'm sorry." He paused, and then added, "For whatever I did back then."

I was stunned as I heard the words coming out of his mouth. I couldn't believe that I was actually getting the apology that I would have wanted so badly in the past, just to have him understand that he had hurt me. I was incredulous that I was getting this chance, that I was looking at Avi across from me and hearing him make amends from so many years ago, directly to my face.

"Thanks, I appreciate that," I said simply in response. I gave him a small smile and then added quickly, "We're good now, don't worry. Let's move on." And I meant it.

As we continued talking and sipping our drinks, I learned that Avi was now working for the Hillel organization in DC, and I told him about my work with the city government. I felt myself having a good time. While we talked and laughed together, I suddenly and accidentally hit the tall, narrow glass in front of me with my hand, completely knocking it over onto the floor, spreading liquid and ice cubes everywhere, which only made both of us laugh even harder. A very short while later, Avi somehow, amazingly, did exactly the same thing; his hand accidentally knocked his drink while we were talking, pouring it all over the table this time. As I watched the spilled beverage run off the wooden surface and begin dripping onto the floor, I imagined how our server must be shaking his head with disapproval, and I was laughing so hard that I had to actively make sure I didn't accidentally pee in my pants. My face hurt. I hadn't laughed that hard in a long time, and it felt awesome. I couldn't believe we had both just literally spilled our entire drinks, one right after the other, as though we were physically incapable of sitting at a table and having beverages and conversation in any kind of civilized manner.

When our laughter eventually died down, I looked at him, still somewhat in disbelief that I was sitting here with Avi, Avi from camp, Avi from nine years ago, at a table at the Bier Baron, a bar that I had been to so many times before, on something that felt kind of like a date. It was starting to get late for a Wednesday, so we soon paid our bill and stepped back outside into the cold night.

"Can I walk you home?" Avi asked, his brow slightly furrowed and a hopeful look in his eyes.

I smiled broadly, pleased that he also felt like we weren't done talking. "Yeah, sure."

We walked slowly back toward the Foggy Bottom neighborhood where I now lived, in step with one another, our breath visible in delicate white clouds in the dark air in front of us as we talked. I looked at Avi and realized with surprise that he was shorter than I remembered. He had seemed so tall back at camp, so much older and more worldly than my nineteen-year-old self. But now, he was just a guy. A thirty-two-year-old man who had lived through some things and survived some trials but had fought back to continue on a life path of his choosing. It struck me also, though, how very human Avi seemed to me now. When I was nineteen he had felt larger than life.

When we reached the corner where I had to turn onto my block, we stopped as I gestured down the street. "Well, I'm this way."

Avi and I looked at each other and smiled, both of us visibly dawdling to buy time. His grin was boyish, and I saw some of the old familiar mischievousness in his eyes, which now displayed genuine uncertainty as his brow wrinkled.

"Can I . . . kiss you?" he asked, and I smiled wider.

"Yeah."

We stood there on the street corner in an embrace, and I felt his full lips on mine, a welcome source of warmth in the cold air. As we kissed, in an instant I was back on the old 1970s striped couch in the staff lounge at Camp Laurelwood in Connecticut. We were older now, and better kissers, but I was struck by how completely familiar it was to kiss him. With his lips on mine, I felt like I was revisiting a place that I had been before that I didn't know I remembered. Everything felt exactly the same. The taste, the feel, the way our lips and tongues interacted. I didn't know you could remember a person by their kiss until that moment.

We pulled apart at a natural break, both of us smiling as we said goodnight. I turned the corner and walked slowly toward my apartment, unable to suppress a smile to myself, still reliving the moment of kissing him on that couch when I was nineteen and he was twenty-three and our whole adult lives were still ahead of us.

I stuck my hands into my pockets to shield them from the cold as I continued walking, sighing deeply. I felt completely content by how the evening had gone, but I knew that while I had had a great time with Avi and the kiss was lovely, it was all significant mostly because of the nostalgia that came with it, because it brought me back to another place, to an earlier time. Other than that, and the magnificence of the apology that had been nine years in the making, nothing about our interaction had felt truly extraordinary. I felt like we had gotten along as friends, and I knew deep down that even if we tried to go out again, that was eventually what we were going to remain. I had a feeling he perceived something similar.

As I continued up the steps to my apartment, I felt satisfied with the experience I had had with Avi. It was the ending that we needed, and I was fortunate to have been given the opportunity to reconnect with him after all those years and to have that apology, that closure. I thought about how I had only planned to stay out for a very short time that Thursday night at the bocce team happy hour but how something inside me had just said "Oh, what the hell," and completely against everything that made sense for me that week, I chose not to go home quite yet and went to the other restaurant anyway. And then I ran into Avi, and it was as though circumstances beyond our control had brought us into the same space that night.

Avi had been living in the same city as me for a few years before we connected that evening, just as Jared had been residing in nearly the same neighborhood as me for a time before we spontaneously reconnected on the street that night a couple years before, right after I had been thinking about him. And recently, I had heard Sam's voice, a voice from my college days, singing to me through my TV screen, hurdling over geographic boundaries, barreling through the limits of the years that had passed us by, in order to reach me just when I needed to hear it.

As I approached the door to my apartment building, I turned and looked back at the street, wondering who else I might be nearly crossing paths with on a regular basis in this large but often seemingly small city, like two characters in a video game careening on our independent journeys within the city labyrinth, nearly bouncing into each other on occasion, each time quickly spinning off in different directions because it was not yet the right moment for our paths to intertwine. As I pulled out my keys, I exhaled and saw my breath in the night air in front of me, my lips still tingling from the end of a kiss that had begun nine years before.

AFTERWORD

Thanks for reading! If you enjoyed this book and have a moment to spare, I would really appreciate a short review, as this can help new readers find the book and decide if it's right for them.

SOUNDTRACK

Want more *And Again, It's You*? There's a Spotify playlist! Relive the book through music with a mixture of songs that played on my computer, iPod, or in my head during the time periods in the book, plus songs from the years since that called some *And Again, It's You* moments to mind for me. I hope you'll enjoy listening to it as much as I enjoyed compiling it. Find it at spoti.fi/31QbY9n.

ACKNOWLEDGMENTS

I would like to sincerely thank Dan Harris, Bethany Perskie, Rachel Orgel, Steve Jacobs, and Daniel Shorstein for reviewing early (sorry) and late drafts of this book; without your comments and insight I would not have reached this stage. Another special thank you to Dan Harris for your sage author-ly advice throughout this entire process.

Thank you to Shelby Newsom for your steadfast editing work, Bailey McGinn for crafting a cover design that perfectly matched what I was trying to say, and Danna Mathias Steele for your beautiful interior layout.

Most importantly, thank you to my parents for raising me to believe that I could be anything that I wanted, and to Daniel Shorstein for not only your creative contributions throughout this process, but also your love, support, encouragement, and assumption of additional household responsibilities.

Finally, to the individuals who served as the basis for this book, thank you for enriching my life in a way that inspired me.

CPSIA information can be obtained
at www.ICGtesting.com
Printed in the USA
LVHW040040221222
735706LV00003B/203